Social Security Benefits Handbook

Stanley A. Tomkiel III
Attorney at Law

SPHINX PUBLISHING
Sphinx International, Inc.
Post Office Box 25
Clearwater, FL 34617
Tel: 813-587-0999
Fax: 813-586-5088

SPHINX ®
is a registered trademark of Sphinx International, Inc.

First Edition, 1996

ISBN 1-57248-033-5
Library of Congress Catalog Number: 96-67021

Manufactured in the United States of America.

This publication is designed to provide accurate and authoritative information in regard to the subject matter covered. It is sold with the understanding that the publisher is not engaged in rendering legal, accounting or other professional services. If legal advice or other expert assistance is required, the service of a competent professional person should be sought.

> -From a Declaration of Principles jointly adopted by a Committee of American Bar Association and a Committee of Publishers.

Published by Sphinx Publishing, a division of Sphinx International, Inc., Post Office Box 25, Clearwater, Florida 34617-0025. This publication is available through most book stores but if you cannot find it locally you can order it by mail for $14.95 plus $3.00 shipping. Florida residents please add sales tax. For credit card orders call 1-800-226-5291.

Table of Contents

Chapter 1
The Social Security Administration

§ 101 - In General

The Social Security Administration (SSA) is the branch of the Federal government which has the duty of administering several provisions of the Social Security Act. The Social Security Administration (SSA) was under the jurisdiction of the Department of Health and Human Services until March 1995, when it became an independent agency. The Social Security Act provides for the payment of monthly benefits to retired and disabled workers and their dependents and to certain survivors of covered workers who are deceased. Social Security also provides for Medicare and other programs such as Supplemental Security Income and Black Lung benefits. The benefits referred to as Social Security benefits, however, are those monthly benefits payable to retired workers, disabled workers, and the survivors of covered workers. Because regular Social Security benefits are based on the earnings of covered workers, SSA also keeps track of the earnings of almost all American workers.

There are presently approximately 43 million people throughout the United States who receive monthly checks from SSA and there are approximately 141 million covered workers whose wages are recorded by the Social Security Administration each year. The Social Security Administration is one of the largest government agencies.

SSA is divided into many different bureaus and branches to accomplish all its duties. The main offices are located in Baltimore, Maryland. The entire United States is divided up by SSA into districts, each of which has its own District Office. Many of these District Offices also have branch offices. There are seven hundred (700) district and branch offices throughout the nation. The District Office is designed to handle all contact with members of the public. Most dealings you may have with SSA normally will be done through your local District Office.

This chapter will discuss the different bureaus and their general functions and will discuss the different types of District Office employees with whom you will come in contact.

§ 102 - Internal Offices

The Social Security Administration (SSA) makes contact with members of the public through District Offices and Teleservice Centers (see §§ 103 and 105 below). However, much of the work of SSA is done by people in offices which have no contact with the public. We will discuss some of these major offices that the public never sees. These are referred to as internal offices.

Central Office (CO). The main office of SSA is called the Central Office. It is the headquarters of SSA and is located in Baltimore, Maryland. The Central Office issues all regulations and instruction to the District Offices. It interprets the law, and issues policy statements.

Office of Central Records Operations (OCRO). This office deals with the huge volume of information necessary to perform the duties of the Social Security Administration. Its main functions include the assigning of Social Security numbers to workers, keeping track of changes of names on Social Security records, and maintaining the records of earnings reported by employers for each individual Social Security number. This office is also located in Baltimore, Maryland.

When a person files a claim for Social Security benefits, the District Office where the claim is being handled must contact the Office of Central Records Operations to obtain the earnings record of the worker.

Program Service Centers (PSC). There are six Program Service Centers located throughout the United States. These offices process claims that cannot be processed by the District Office. They also process reinstatement of benefits after they have been suspended or terminated. After a claim has been processed in a district office it is sent to the Program Service Center for storage and further processing. The claims folders are generally assigned to the different program service centers based on the Social Security number of the wage earner on whose earnings the claim is based. The names and addresses of the different program service centers, along with the breakdown of their claims numbers is listed in Appendix 12. Sometimes the Program Service Center will have direct contact with beneficiaries. They handle such things as student reports, annual report of earnings and overpayment notices. Any information requested from a Program Service Center can be returned directly or can be returned through a local District Office, whichever you prefer.

Office of Disability Operations (ODO). This office is similar to a Program Service Center, but it handles cases based on disability benefits. If a worker who is disabled is age fifty-nine or older, his file is maintained in the Program Service Center instead of the Office of Disability Operations. When the person turns sixty-five his disability benefit is automatically converted to a retirement benefit by the Program Service Center. This conversion to a retirement benefit is only a technicality; the amount of the benefit does not change. The files of disabled workers under age fifty-nine are kept in the Office of Disability Operations. This office is also located in Baltimore, Maryland.

Division of International Operations (DIO). This office is similar to a Program Service Center, but it covers cases where beneficiaries reside outside of the United States. It is also located in Baltimore, Maryland.

Regional Offices (RO). The entire United States is divided into ten regions by the Social Security Administration. Each region has a Regional Office which deals directly with the Central Office and then deals with the local District Offices within the region. An individual District Office in the region does not have direct contact with Central Office. Instead it deals through the Regional Office. The Regional Office is staffed with experts in all areas of Social Security. Regional offices also review the District Offices to make sure that they are applying the rules and regulations of Social Security consistently.

§ 103 - Telephone Services

Teleservice Center (TSC) and Telephone Service. The Social Security Administration (SSA) has set up special centers designed to handle telephone inquiries from members of the public. These are called Teleservice Centers (TSC). They are designed to take the burden of voluminous phone calls away from the District Office. The nation-wide toll free number is 1-800-772-1213. Service representatives handle calls from 7 a.m. to 7 p.m. Pre-recorded information and services are available after hours. Hearing impaired callers with TDD equipment can call 1-800-325-0778 between 7 a.m. and 7 p.m. Medicare information is available from 8 a.m. to 8 p.m. Eastern time at 1-800-638-6833.

The Teleservice Centers are staffed by Service Representatives (§ 105). They have computer terminals available to obtain the computer records of all beneficiaries who have been established on the computer (§ 104). They are able to handle changes of address, and reports of missing checks. If a claim has been recently filed and has not yet been set up on the computer system, you will be referred to the local District Office where the claim is being handled. That phone number was given to you at the time you filed your initial application on the receipt form that Social Security gives everyone who files a claim. The Teleservice Centers can also provide general information about Social Security, although it is recommended that you speak with a Claims Representative if the question is out of the ordinary or is complex.

District Office Telephone Service. Many District Offices have telephone service available to file claims, report changes of address or missing checks and obtain information regarding Social Security. Almost all business you may have with the Social Security office can be handled over the telephone. You can even file a claim on the phone. Many District Offices have what is referred to as a teleclaims unit. These units are staffed by Claims Representatives who will obtain the necessary information from you over the phone, complete the application form and mail it to you for your review and signature. It is against the policy of many Social Security offices to send out blank application forms. If you call them up to file a claim, you will have to give the information over the phone, so that the Claims Representative can properly fill out the application. This is done to ensure that there is no misunderstanding of information and that all the information and required evidence is obtained.

§ 104 - Computer System

SSADARS (pronounced "SAY-DARS"), is the basic computer system of the Social Security Administration (SSA). It links all District Offices nationwide. It allows personnel in the local District Office to make computer inputs to establish claims on the rolls and to make any necessary changes, such as change of address or reports of missing checks. Records of individual beneficiaries are stored on the computer system. Such things as payment amounts, addresses, beneficiaries on record and so forth, may be obtained from the computer. All District Offices have "on-line" terminals to the SSADARS. This means that they can obtain the information almost immediately. Unfortunately, no computer system is perfect and sometimes the system is "down." When this happens the personnel in the District Office cannot get the information immediately.

When claims can be processed through the SSADARS, the time frames for processing are greatly reduced. Unfortunately, not all claims can be processed this way, but the majority are. For claims which cannot go through the system, manual processing at a Program Service Center is required (§ 106). This adds significantly to the time required for processing. A claim going through the computer system can take as little as fifteen days. A claim going through manual processing may take up to three months or more.

§ 105 - The District Office (DO)

The entire United States is divided geographically by the Social Security Administration (SSA) into many hundreds of districts. There are over 1,100 district and branch offices throughout the United States. Each district or branch office is responsible for dealing with all members of the public who reside in that district. Any business you may have to conduct with SSA will be done through your local District Office. You may determine where your District Office is located by looking in the telephone book under United States Government, Health and Human Services, Social Security Administration. You may deal with any District Office you prefer. If another District Office is more convenient than your own local District Office, you may ask that your case be handled at the other one.

District Offices are open during regular business hours. The exact times of opening and closing change from one office to another. Some offices open at 8:00 a.m. and close at 4:30 p.m. Other offices open at 8:30 a.m. and close at 5:00 p.m. Most of your business with Social Security can be conducted over the telephone without having to go in person to the District Office, (see § 105).

If you wish to visit your district office in person, you cannot usually make an appointment. Visitors at the district office are taken on a first-come, first-served basis.

Best times to visit the District Office. Sometimes you can visit a District Office and be served immediately. Other times you may have to wait for over an hour or more. It all depends on how crowded the office is when you get there. The volume of visitors to District Offices usually follows a pattern and if you go at a time when it is not crowded you will be served more promptly. Generally speaking, you are better off going to your District Office towards the end of a month. The first week to ten days is usually the busiest in a District Office. It is at these times that you may encounter a wait of an hour or more. The reason is that Social Security checks are paid on the third day of the month. Supplemental Security Income checks (§ 1401) are paid on the first day of the month. Each month there are many people who do not receive their checks, or have had them stolen. Therefore district offices are usually crowded during the first week to ten days of any given month.

Generally the latter part of the week is less busy than the early part of the week. Mondays are usually very busy, whereas Fridays are slow.

The District Offices are busy during lunchtime. This is because many people who work go there at their own lunchtime and also because the Social Security employees have to eat, too. Interviewers at the Social Security office have staggered lunch hours so that at least half of them will be on duty during this time. However, because the other half is out to lunch the lines can grow and you may encounter delays at this time. Likewise, the employees at the District Office take coffee breaks. They receive a fifteen-minute coffee break in the afternoon. Again, these breaks are staggered, but at around 10:00 a.m. and around 3:00 p.m., half of the interviewers are on their coffee breaks.

Processing Units. The business handled by the District Office is divided into different units. Each unit is staffed by one or more employees. Among interviewers, the basic division is between claims units and service units. Claims units handle initial applications and the more complex areas of Social Security rules. They are staffed by Claims Representatives. The service units handle what are referred to as "post-entitlement" issues. These are the events that occur after you have become entitled to checks, such as changes of address, reports of missing checks, annual reports of earnings, and so forth. Service units are staffed by Service Representatives. A Service Representative is not able to handle an initial claim.

Generally, there is a special unit set up in each District Office to handle disability related cases and a special unit for Supplemental Security Income cases (§ 1401). In larger offices the work will be further divided among the Claims Representatives and Service Representatives based on an alphabetical breakdown.

Each Claims Representative and Service Representative will be assigned a certain part of the alphabet and the cases of all persons with names that fall within that part of the alphabet will be assigned to that particular Claims Representative or Service Representative. That worker will handle the paper work for the claim, but may interview people regardless of the alphabetical breakdown.

The different Claims Representatives and Service Representatives are periodically re-assigned to different alphabetical breakdowns, so do not be surprised to find that a different Claims Representative is handling your case a few months later.

The different types of employees that you come in contact with at the local District Office will be discussed later in this chapter.

In addition to District Offices, the Social Security Administration also sets up Branch Offices and contact stations. The Branch Office is a smaller version of the District Office and comes under its jurisdiction. It is staffed with the same types of employees found in the District Office. The manager of a Branch Office reports to the manager of the District Office with which it is associated.

The contact station is not a regular office. It is simply a place where a Field Representative or a Claims Representative will go on a periodic basis to service people in outlying areas. They are usually set up in areas where the jurisdiction of the District Office is large. The Field Representative will go to the contact station at set times, such as the third Tuesday of the month, for example. All paper work is taken back to the District Office and processed there by the regular personnel according to the alphabetic breakdown.

If you live far from your local District Office, you should find out if a contact station is set up closer to you and when the Social Security representative will be there. Contact Stations are commonly established in municipal buildings or senior citizen centers.

District Office Personnel In General

Each District Office is staffed with many different types of employees, each one handling specific functions. Every District Office has a district manager who is the highest authority in the office. He is not usually involved with the technical aspects of Social Security, such as deciding claims. His duties are basically administrative, such as maintaining personnel records and making sure the office work moves along quickly. He also deals with Congressmen and Senators who make inquiries on behalf of their constituents (§ 1014). The District Manager is the person to contact in the District Office if you wish to praise a particular employee for a job well done or to complain about an employee for poor service.

Generally, the district manager does not deal with the public on a regular basis. The employees who deal with the public regularly are Claims Representatives, Service Representatives, Field Representatives, and the receptionist. In addition to these employees who have public contact, there are supervisors, clericals and technical employees who deal with the paper work and the computers. If you visit your local Social Security office and have to wait because all the interviewers are tied up interviewing people, you may see a number of employees sitting at a desk not interviewing anyone. Do not be upset, these are probably the non-interviewing personnel.

The Receptionist

When you go to your District Office, you will be greeted at the front desk by the receptionist. She will ask your name and ask a few questions to determine the nature of your visit. It is her job to determine which employee should service you. At the District Office, different types of business are handled by different employees.

In addition to the reception duties, the receptionist usually handles matters dealing with Social Security numbers, such as assigning new numbers or changing your name for the Social Security records. The receptionist has little training other than that and it is not a good idea to take advice on anything else from the receptionist. Some overzealous receptionists have been known to give erroneous information about Social Security matters. It is wise to take your advice only from a Claims Representative or Service Representative.

After taking your name and determining the nature of your visit, the receptionist will generally ask you to be seated and will assign you to the next available representative who handles your type of case. It is possible that other persons who have arrived after you will be taken care of first because a representative who handles their type of business is available before a representative who handles your type of business.

The Claims Representative (CR)

The Claims Representative position is perhaps the single most important position in the entire Social Security organization. It is the responsibility of the Claims Representative to be knowledgeable about all aspects of the Social Security regulations. The duty of the Claims Representative has two sides. One aspect is to represent the Social Security Administration (SSA) and the other aspect is to assist claimants who are making claims for benefits under the Social Security program. The major responsibility of the Claims Representative, of course, has to do with initial claims for benefits. The Claims Representative interviews a prospective claimant, determines the type of claim he or she should be making and completes the appropriate claims forms.

The Claims Representative also determines what documents, evidence, or other information is required to successfully prosecute the claim and advises the claimant accordingly. The Claims Representative also will take steps to obtain the necessary information or documents. Additionally, on many of these initial claims, the Claims Representative makes the decision to pay or to deny the claim. In addition to these claims duties, the Claims Representative is also responsible for making determinations relating to representative payees (§1414) for incompetent beneficiaries, for making determinations of the proper amount of wages which are subject to Social Security, and for making recommendations about whether or not overpayments may be waived in particular cases. It is also the duty of the Claims Representative to provide the public with information about the Social Security rules, regulations and procedures.

In theory, the Claims Representative knows everything about all of the various aspects of Social Security. This knowledge is not gained in a short period of time however, and in a given District Office there will be Claims Representatives with varying degrees of experience. The person who becomes a Claims Representative is considered to be a trainee for three years in that position because it takes at least that long to get a good working knowledge of all the rules and regulations involved with the job. It takes at least another year of experience to become fully versed in all the aspects of Social Security for which the Claims Representative is responsible.

The majority of seasoned Claims Representatives are thoroughly knowledgeable professionals who are well versed in all aspects of Social Security law and regulations. There are some exceptions to that general statement. Because of the very complex and technical nature of the area, a number of Claims Representatives, even though they are on the job for many years, are still not thoroughly competent. Just as there are incompetent doctors and lawyers, there are incompetent Claims Representatives. If you believe that the Claims Representative with whom you are dealing is giving you erroneous or inaccurate information, ask him to show you in the program operations manual the authority for his statement (see §106). If you are still not satisfied, you should then ask to speak to an operations supervisor to double check.

The Service Representative (SR)

As noted above, there are two basic types of employees who interview the public - Claims Representatives and Service Representatives. The Claims Representative is discussed above. Basically the Service Representative deals with "post-entitlement" aspects of Social Security. Post-entitlement has to do with things that affect people who are already receiving benefits.

Changes of address, reports of missing checks, annual report of earnings, refunds of overpayments, and Medicare claims are the most common things with which the Service Representative deals. These employees are also well versed in the "retirement test," also known as the earnings limitations. The "retirement test" is used to determine how earnings affect benefits. This is fully discussed in Chapter 8.

Service Representatives do not handle claims, payee determinations, changes to the earnings record or other complex areas of Social Security.

The workload in a District Office is divided among the Service Representatives according to an alphabetical breakdown. Beneficiaries are assigned to Service Representatives based on their last names. For example, a Service Representative may be assigned the letters "A" through "E." If your name begins with an "A" through an "E," your case will be assigned to that Service Representative.

The Service Representatives are periodically re-assigned to different alphabetical breakdowns. You may not always have the same Service Representative assigned to your case each time you go to the District Office. The alphabetical breakdowns are used only for paper work processing. Interviewers may be assigned without regard to alphabetical breakdowns if this is required to avoid delays.

The job of the Service Representative requires a thorough knowledge of complicated rules and procedures. Most Service Representatives are very competent. Unfortunately, some are not. If you question the accuracy of information or advice from a Service Representative, you should ask him or her to show you in the claims manual or programs operations manual (§106) the authority for the information. If you are still not satisfied, you may ask to speak to an operations supervisor.

The Field Representative (FR)

Each District and Branch Office has at least one Field Representative. A Field Representative is basically a Claims Representative who goes out of the office when the need arises. This usually occurs when a claimant or beneficiary is homebound or in a hospital. The Field Representative makes speeches before groups and visits contact stations. The Field Representative does not usually process the paper work himself. He brings it back to the District Office where it is assigned to the appropriate Claims Representative or Service Representative according to the alphabetical breakdown, as discussed above.

If you belong to a group or an organization which would like to hear a speaker on Social Security matters, you can call your local District Office and ask the Field Representative to make a speech. Field Representatives frequently work at night and on weekends for these purposes. The Field Representative's broad-based knowledge is usually sufficient to answer all general questions.

§ 106 - The Programs Operations Manual System (POMS)

The Programs Operations Manual System (POMS) is the rulebook used by all District Office personnel. These manuals are issued by the Central Office and provide the working rules and interpretations of the law and regulations. The official regulations of the Social Security Administration (SSA) published in the Federal Register and available in law libraries are almost never used by the personnel in the District Offices. Instead, they rely almost exclusively upon the POMS. The POMS is available in every District Office for review by members of the public. Generally, the policy of the Social Security office is to require an interviewer to be present while a member of the public reviews the POMS. This is required because much of the language is written in bureaucratic shorthand which can be meaningless to you. A Claims Representative or Service Representative will be required to interpret this bureaucratic language. The POMS is the "Bible" of Social Security and all decisions must be founded upon the provisions contained in these manuals. If you doubt the accuracy of information given to you by any Social Security interviewer, you should ask to see where it is stated in the POMS. The interviewer should be able to locate the pertinent section to show you in black and white.

Chapter 2
Eligibility Requirements

§ 207.7	Exceptions to the Nine Month Duration of Marriage Requirement for Widow's Benefits
§ 207.8	The "Child in Care" Requirement
§ 207.9	The Child Relationship Requirement
§ 207.10	Dependency Requirements: Children and Grandchildren

§ 201 - In General

The Social Security Act provides for the payment of many different types of benefits. Each type of benefit has specific eligibility requirements which a claimant must meet in order to receive the benefit. The requirements of the different types of benefits are stated in the following sections. Once a person becomes entitled to a benefit, it may not be paid because earnings are in excess of the applicable limits or for other reasons. This chapter deals only with the basic eligibility requirements. Earnings as they affect the payment of benefits will be discussed in Chapter 8, Earnings Limitations. Also, almost all benefits require an application to be filed by the claimant. Application requirements are discussed in full in Chapter 4. Each type of benefit requires that the worker on whose record the benefits are based have what is called an "insured status." This means that he or she has enough work credits. There are different kinds of insured status. Some require more work than others. These different types of insured status will be discussed in detail in Chapter 6. This chapter will deal in detail only with eligibility requirements other than the application requirements and the insured status requirement. The amount of the actual benefit the beneficiary will receive will be discussed in detail in Chapter 7, Benefit Amounts.

The benefits usually referred to as Social Security benefits are provided under the basic programs of the Social Security Act. These are Retirement Insurance, Survivors Insurance, Disability Insurance, and Health Insurance.

Disabled and retired workers, their wives and young children, are paid monthly benefits if they meet the eligibility requirements discussed in this chapter. Under survivors insurance, widows and young children are paid monthly benefits if they meet the eligibility requirements discussed in this chapter.

Benefits are also payable to certain divorced wives and divorced widows and to certain parents of covered workers. There are many different kinds of monthly benefits. We have categorized fifteen different types of benefits in this chapter. Eligibility requirements for each is listed separately. In addition to monthly benefits, the Social Security Act also provides for Medicare. This is officially called Health Insurance and has two parts - Hospital Insurance and Medical Insurance. This is discussed more fully in Chapter 12 - Medicare. We list in this chapter the eligibility requirements.

We do not discuss eligibility requirements for other programs which are administered by Social Security such as Supplemental Security Income (§1401) or Black Lung benefits (§1402). We deal only with the regular Social Security benefits in this chapter.

§ 202 - Retirement Benefits

Other Names: Old Age Insurance Benefits; Retirement Insurance Benefits.

Beneficiary Identification Code (§1407) : A

Requirements:
1. You are at least age 62 throughout the month, (§207.4).
2. You have enough work covered by Social Security to be "fully insured" (§602).
3. You file an application (see Chapter 4).

Benefit Amount: 100% of the Primary Insurance Amount (§702.1) at age 65, reduced for age before 65. (See Chapter 7 for a full discussion.)

Termination: Entitlement ends with the month before the month of death (§1009).

§ 203 - Disability Benefits

Other Names: Disability Insurance Benefits; Disabled Worker Benefits.

Beneficiary Identification Code (§1407) : HA

Requirements:
1. You are under age 65, (a full unreduced retirement benefit is paid at age 65 instead of disability benefits, even if you are disabled).
2. You have enough work covered by Social Security to meet the special disability insured status (§604).
3. You file an application (see Chapter 4).

4. You are totally disabled (§502).
5. You have been totally disabled for at least five months (§507).

Benefit Amount: 100% of the Primary Insurance Amount (§702.1) not reduced for age. (See Chapter 7 for a full discussion of computations of benefits and see §511 and §512 for the effect of workers compensation benefits or other disability benefits. The disability benefit is subject to offset in some cases).

Termination: Entitlement ends with:
1. The month before you turn age 65. (You are automatically switched to Retirement benefits).
2. The second month after the disability ceases (§513).
3. The month before the month of death (§1009).

§ 204 - Spouse's Benefits

§ 204.1 - Spouse's Benefits: Age 62 and Older

Other Names: Wife's Benefits; Husband's Benefits (depending on sex), Aged Spouse, Aged Wife, Aged Husband.

Beneficiary Identification Code (§1407): B (or HB if the worker received disability benefits)

Requirements:
1. You are the wife or husband of a worker entitled to retirement or disability benefits. Note: the marriage may be "deemed valid" by SSA even if it is not legally recognized, see §207.5.
2. Your marriage lasted for at least one year, (see §207.6 for exceptions to this requirement).
3. You are at least age 62 throughout the month (§207.4).
4. You file an application (Chapter 4).
5. You are not entitled to a higher retirement or disability benefit on your own earnings record. (You may be entitled to some spouse's benefits even if you are entitled on your own record, if your benefit is lower than one half of your spouse's Primary Insurance Amount (see §302).

Benefit Amount: one-half of your spouse's Primary Insurance Amount (§702.1) at age 65 reduced for age before 65 (§703.1) unless you have a child in your care (§207.8); reduced by your own benefit (see §302); and subject to the family maximum. See Chapter 7 for a full discussion.

Termination: Entitlement ends with:

1. The month before you become entitled to a higher benefit on your own account (see §302).
2. The month before you become divorced (you may be able to switch over to divorced spouse's benefit - §204.2).
3. The month before the spouse on whose earnings you receive benefits dies or is no longer disabled [in the event of death you may switch to a widow(er)'s benefit (see §204.4 for requirements and see §405 for automatic conversion from spouse's to widow(er)'s benefits].
4. If your benefits are based on a "deemed" marriage, (see §207.5), the month before you marry someone else or the legal wife of the worker becomes entitled on his account.
5. The month before the month of death (§1009).

Other: Spouse's benefits are now gender neutral. You may be eligible either as the husband or the wife of the worker. Whenever the term wife's benefits is used in this book, you may substitute husband's benefits if applicable.

§ 204.2 - Spouse's Benefits: With Child in Care

Other Names: Young Wife; Young Husband; Young Spouse

Beneficiary Identification Code (§1407): B2 (or HB2 if the worker receives disability benefits)

Requirements: The requirements are the same as an aged spouse, (§204.1), with one exception. You may collect at any age as long as you have a child of the worker in your care (§207.8) who is entitled to child benefits on the worker's account and who is either under age 16 or a disabled child of any age for whom you are rendering personal services (§§205.1 - 205.4 for who qualifies as children).

Benefit Amount: 50% of the spouse's Primary Insurance Amount (§702). There is no reduction for being under age 65. The benefit is subject to reduction for the family maximum (see Chapter 7 for a full discussion of computations).

Termination: Occurs the same as for aged spouse's benefits (see §204.1), and when the youngest child turns 16 (see §207.8).

Other: Spouse's benefits are gender neutral. You may be entitled whether you are the wife or the husband of the covered worker.

Note: the benefits may be suspended for any month you do not have a child in your care (§207.8, "Child in Care" and §1008, Suspension of Benefits).

§ 204.3 - Spouse's Benefits: Divorced Spouse

Other Names: Divorced Wife, Divorced Husband.

Beneficiary Identification Code (§1407) : B6

Requirements:
1. Your ex-spouse (the worker) is entitled to retirement or disability benefits. Note that beginning January 1985, A divorced spouse may be "independently entitled" if divorced at least two years. This means the divorced spouse may receive benefits even though the worker has not yet filed or his benefits are being suspended because of excess earnings. The two year requirement is designed to avoid any incentive for divorce solely to take advantage of this provision. If the ex-spouse has not filed, he must be "eligible"; he must be "insured" (see Chapter 6) and age 62 or disabled.
2. You are the wife or husband of the worker as defined by SSA (§207.5).
3. You had been married to the worker for at least ten years immediately before the divorce became final (you cannot add up the years married to one man if you were divorced and then re-married to the same man).
4. You file an application (see Chapter 4).
5. You are age 62 throughout the month (§207.4). You cannot be entitled as a divorced wife if you are under age 62 even if you do have a child in your care.
6. You are not entitled to a higher retirement or disability benefit on your own account (§302).
7. You are unmarried.

Benefit Amount : same as aged spouse (§204.1), but not subject to the Family Maximum.

Termination: Entitlement ends with:
1. The same conditions for an aged wife (§204.1).
2. When you re-marry. However, you may continue to be eligible if you re-marry certain other Social Security beneficiaries (§904).

§ 204.4 - Spouse's Benefits: Widow, Age 60 and Over

Other Names: Widow's Insurance Benefit, Widower's Insurance Benefit, Aged Widow, Aged Widower.

Beneficiary Identification Code (§1407): D
Requirements:
1. The worker to whom you were married died fully insured (see Chapter 6).
2. You were "married" (§207.5, The Marriage Requirement) to the worker.
3. You were married for at least nine months before the worker died (see §207.7 for exceptions to this requirement).
4. You file an application (see Chapter 4, especially §405, for automatic conversion from wife to widow).
5. You are at least age 60.
6. You are not actually entitled to a higher retirement or disability benefit on your own account (§303).
7. You are not married (if you re-marry after age 60 then you are not married for Social Security purposes).

Benefit Amount: 100% of the worker's Primary Insurance Amount §702 reduced for age, if you take it before 65, also subject to other reductions, see Chapter 7. See Chapter 3 if you also worked on your own account, especially §303.

Termination: Entitlement ends with:
1. The month before you become entitled to a higher retirement or disability benefit on your own account (see §303 for a discussion of dual entitlement).
2. If you are entitled based on a deemed marriage (§207.5) benefits will end if another person becomes entitled as the legal widow or widower.
3. The month before the month of death (§1009).

Other: Widow's benefits are gender neutral.

§ 204.5 - Spouse's Benefits: Mother and Widow with Child Care

Other Names: Young Widow, Mother's Benefits, Father's Benefits.

Beneficiary Identification Code (§1407): E

Requirements:
1. The worker died fully or currently insured (see Chapter 6).
2. You were "married" to the worker (§207.5).
3. You file an application (see Chapter 4, especially §405).
4. You are unmarried.
5. You are not entitled to a higher widow's benefits on another account or to a higher retirement or disability benefit on your own account (see Chapter 3, Dual Entitlement).
6. You have a "child in your care" (§207.8).

Benefit Amount: 75% of the worker's Primary Insurance Amount (§702) subject to the family maximum (see Chapter 7).

Termination: Entitlement ends with the month before the month in which any of the following occur (see §1009 for a general discussion of termination of benefits):
1. You become entitled to a higher benefit on another account.
2. The child in your care turns 16 unless the child is disabled and you are rendering services for that child (see §207.8, The Child in Care Requirement). If you are entitled because you have a disabled adult child in your care, the benefits will end if the child is no longer disabled.
3. You re-marry (for exceptions if you re-marry another Social Security beneficiary, see §904).
4. If your entitlement is based on a deemed marriage (§207.5), and another person becomes entitled on the account as the legal widow.
5. The month before the month of death.

Other: If your benefits end because you have re-married they may be reinstated if the subsequent marriage is terminated (§904). Benefits are gender neutral.

§ 204.6 - Spouse's Benefits: Disabled Widow's Benefits; Age 50 to 59

Other Names: Disabled Widow's Insurance Benefit, Disabled Widower's Insurance Benefit.

Beneficiary Identification Code (§1407) : W

Requirements: the requirements are the same as for an aged widow (§204.4) except that instead of being 60 you meet the following requirements:
1. You are at least age 50.

2. You are totally disabled (§502).
3. The disability started not later than seven years after the worker's death or seven years after you were last entitled to mother's benefits (§204.5) or disabled widow's benefits, if you were previously entitled.
4. The disability lasts for more than five months (§507) and is expected to last at least one year (§502).

Benefit Amount: 71% of the worker's Primary Insurance Amount (§702). Before 1984 there was additional reduction for age for each month under age 60. This is now eliminated. See Chapter 7 for a dull discussion of computations of benefits.

Termination: Entitlement ends with the same events as the Widow (§204.4), and when the disability ends (see §513). Note that for the Disabled Widow, re-marriage after age 50 is not considered for Social Security purposes, beginning in 1984.

Other: Disabled Widow's benefits are gender neutral.

§ 204.7 - Spouse's Benefits: Divorced Widow's Benefits

Other Names: Surviving Divorced Wife, Surviving Divorced Husband, Divorced Widower, Divorced Mother, Divorced Father.

Beneficiary Identification Code (§1407): D6 (divorced aged widow); E1 (divorced young widow - child in care); W6 (disabled divorced widow).

Requirements:
1. The worker died fully insured (for a young widow; currently insured) (See Chapter 6).
2. You were legally married (note that the "deemed valid" marriage is not sufficient (§207.5).
3. The marriage lasted for at least ten years immediately before the divorce.
4. You file an application. (See Chapter 4).
5. You are age 60, or disabled (§502), or have a child of the worker in your care (§207.8).
6. You are not entitled to a higher retirement or disabled benefit on your own account (§303).
7. You are unmarried.

Benefit Amount: Same as for a non-divorced widow, but not subject to the Family Maximum.

Termination: Entitlement ends under the same conditions described in §204.4 for an aged widow, §204.6 for a disabled widow, or §204.5 for a young widow.

§ 205 - Children's Benefits

§ 205.1 - Children's Benefits: Under Age 18

Other Names: Surviving Child, Dependent Child.

Beneficiary Identification Code (§1407): C (HC if the worker receives disability benefits)

Requirements:
1. The worker is entitled to retirement or disability benefits, or, in the case of survivors, died either fully insured (§602) or currently insured (§603).
2. You are the child of the worker as defined in §207.9 below. Under certain circumstances this can include stepchildren, illegitimate children, adopted children, and grandchildren.
3. You are dependent on the worker at the time he becomes eligible for retirement or disability benefits or dies (§207.10). Note that if you are the natural child of the worker, you are deemed dependent.
4. You file an application (see Chapter 4).
5. You are unmarried.
6. You are under age 18 (see §205.2 for students and §205.3 for disabled adult children).

Benefit Amount: Children entitled on a living worker's account receive 50% of the Primary Insurance Amount (§702.1). Children entitled on a deceased worker's account receive 75% of the Primary Insurance Amount. In all cases it is subject to the family maximum (see Chapter 7 for a full discussion of computations).

Termination: Entitlement ends with the month before any of the following events occur (§1009):
1. You turn 18 (unless you are a student or disabled, see §205.2 and §205.3).
2. You marry.

3. The worker's entitlement ends for a reason other than death. If the worker dies, you will be converted to a survivor benefit as a child.
4. You die.

§ 205.2 - Children's Benefits: High School Student

Requirements:
1. The requirements are the same as for a child under age 18, except that you do not have to be under age 18.
2. You must be no older than age 19. Benefits may continue for up to three months after age nineteen if you turn 19 during the school quarter or semester.
3. You must be a full time student in an approved elementary or secondary school.
4. You must not be paid by your employer to attend school.

Benefit Amount: Same as for a child under 18 (§205.1).

Termination: Same as for a child under 18 (§205.1); or if you are no longer a full time student; or you start to be paid by your employer to attend school).

Other: Note that certain college students up to age 22 may continue to be eligible for benefits through April 1985. These benefits are being phased out (§1415).
A school is considered approved if it is accredited by the state in which it is located and its primary purpose is to provide secondary or elementary education. "Full time" means twenty hours per week and at least a 13-week course.

§ 205.3 - Children's Benefits: Disabled Adult Child

Other Names: Childhood Disability Beneficiary, Adult Disabled Child.

Requirements:
1. The requirements are the same as §205.1, except that you must be age 18 or older.
2. You become totally disabled before you reach age 22 (§502). Note that if your benefits stop when you turn age 18, they may be re-established if you become disabled before age 22.

Benefit Amount - same as for children under age 18 (§205.1).

Termination: Entitlement ends with:

1. Under the same conditions described in §205.1 for children under age 18, except the age requirement. In some cases, marriage to another Social Security beneficiary does not terminate disabled child's benefits (§1009).
2. When the disability ceases (§513). If you become disabled again after the disability ceases, the benefit may resume if you become disabled for the second time within seven years after the month in which your disabled child benefits ended.

§ 205.4 - Child's Benefits: Grandchildren

Other Names: These are referred to as Child's Benefits even though the entitlement is based on a grandchild relationship.

Requirements:
Grandchildren may be eligible for benefits if they meet the requirements for children's benefits discussed in the preceding sections and in addition meet these requirements:

1. You are the child of the covered worker's child (§207.9).
2. Your parents were both either deceased or totally disabled (§502) at the time the grandparent first became entitled to retirement benefits, disability benefits, or died. If the grandparent died after becoming entitled to benefits, you must have met the requirements as of the date he or she became entitled to benefits.
3. The grandchild is dependent on the grandparent (§207.10).

Benefit Amount: The benefit amount of grandchildren's benefits is the same as for regular child's benefits.

Termination: The benefits end under the same conditions as they end for other types of child's benefits.

§ 206 - Parent's Benefits

Note that these benefits are payable only to surviving parents of deceased workers. They are not payable if the worker is alive.

Beneficiary Identification Code (§1407): F

Requirements:
1. The worker died fully insured (§602).

2. You are the natural parent of the worker according to the laws of the state where the worker had a permanent home. If you adopted the worker, you must have adopted him or her before he or she was 16. If you are a stepparent you must have married the worker's natural parent before the worker became 16 years old.
3. You are at least age 62.'
4. You have not married since the worker died.
5. You file an application (see Chapter 4).
6. You are not entitled to a retirement or disability greater than the parent's benefit amount.
7. You received at least one half of your support from the worker at the time he died or became disabled if the disability continued up to the time of death. Note that proof of support must be filed with the Social Security Administration (SSA) within two years of the death of the worker or the date he became eligible for benefits. If this proof is not filed within two years of the worker's death or disability whether or not you are eligible to start receiving benefits at that time, you cannot be eligible at a later date, unless you can establish good cause for not filing it timely. You may also be eligible for an exception provided by the Soldiers and Sailors Civil Relief Act of 1948. It would be wise to consult an attorney if the proof of support was not filed within two years of the worker's death or disability.

Benefit Amount: The amount of the parent's benefit depends on whether there are one of two parent entitled on the account. If there is one eligible parent, the benefit is 82% of the worker's Primary Insurance Amount (§702.1). If there are two eligible parents, it is 75% of the worker's Primary Insurance Amount, payable to each parent. It is subject to reduction for the family maximum (see Chapter 7 for a full discussion of computation of benefits).

§ 207 - Other Requirements

§ 207.1 - Special Age 72 Payments

Other Names: Prouty Benefits

In the 1960s, special legislation was passed to allow for special payments to very elderly people, even if they had not worked under Social Security or if they didn't have enough work to qualify for regular benefits. There are only a handful of beneficiaries throughout the country who are eligible for these payments, almost all of whom are receiving them.

If you did not work at all, you must have attained age 72 before 1968 to be eligible. If you became 72 after 1967, you must have three quarters of coverage (§605.1) for each year after 1966 and before the year you become 72. For men who became age 72 in 1972 or later, and for women who attain age 72 in 1970 or later, the work requirement for "fully insured" status (§602) is the same.

We only mention these benefits in passing for the sake of being complete. These benefits are now almost completely phased out.

§ 207.2 - The Lump Sum Death Payment

A lump sum in the amount of $255.00 is payable to certain survivors of a worker who died fully or currently insured (see Chapter 6). A benefit is paid to only one person (with the exception of children, discussed below) according to the following order of priority:

1. The surviving spouse who was living in the same household with the worker at the time of death.
2. A surviving spouse not living in the same household but potentially entitled to monthly benefits on the deceased worker's account in the month of death.
3. If there are neither of the above, then the payment is made to the surviving children of the worker who are eligible for monthly benefits on the account. All the surviving children split the lump sum death benefit evenly.

Only $255 is paid, even if it is split among the surviving children. If there are no people who fit these categories, there is no lump sum death benefit payable.

The application for this benefit must be filed within two years of the death of the worker.

§ 207.3 - Medicare

In this section we will discuss only the basic eligibility requirements for Medicare. Coverage provisions (what Medicare pays for) are discussed in Chapter 12 and application requirements are discussed in Chapter 4.

Medicare has two parts: Hospital Insurance (Part A) and Medical Insurance (Part B). Hospital Insurance primarily pays for in-patient care and Medical Insurance covers doctor bills. Both parts also cover other charges as well (see Chapter 12). There are limits for filing an application for Medicare coverage. If you do not file timely you may lose coverage and have to pay an extra premium for Medical Insurance (§407).

Hospital Insurance

There are three groups of individuals eligible for Medicare Hospital Insurance. The first group are those age 65 or older who either:

a) Receive any Social Security monthly benefit or Railroad Requirement Board monthly benefit or are eligible for them. An application must be filed for Medicare even if you are still working (§404.3); or

b) Are federal employees with sufficient quarters of coverage (federal employees started having Medicare tax withheld from their paychecks effective January of 1983). There are special provisions to grant credit for those employees for work performed before 1983, if they were employed by the Federal government in January 1984; or

c) Pay a monthly premium and who are either U.S. citizens or lawfully admitted resident aliens who have resided in the United States for five continuous years or more.

The second group eligible for Hospital Insurance are those individuals who are entitled to monthly Social Security disability benefits (including disabled adult children and disabled widows) or disabled federal employees with enough work covered for Medicare purposes. The coverage for these groups begins with the twenty-fifth month of disability, not counting the waiting period (§507).

The third group are those individuals who suffer from End Stage Renal Disease (kidney failure) and who undergo a regular course of dialysis or have a kidney transplant and are either fully or currently insured (§§602 and 603); or are the spouse or former spouse (married at least ten years) of someone who is fully or currently insured; or, if under age twenty-five when kidney failure occurs, the child of a worker who is fully or currently insured.

Note: the spouse or parent of the kidney patient need not be eligible for or collecting Social Security benefits. For example, a wage earner who is age 50 and working full time is not eligible for monthly Social Security benefits but his spouse, or children under 25, can still be entitled to Medicare on his record under this provision.

Medical Insurance

There are three groups of people who are eligible for Medicare Medical Insurance.

The first group are those people age 65 or over who are U.S. citizens (or legal aliens admitted for permanent residence and who have resided in the country for five continuous years or more) and who pay the monthly premium. You do not have to be eligible for Hospital Insurance or any other Social Security benefit to be eligible for medical insurance.

The second group of people are those eligible for Hospital Insurance on the basis of disability (see above) who pay the monthly premium.

The third group are those entitled to Medicare Hospital Insurance for the End Stage Renal Disease (see above), and who pay the monthly premium.

§ 207.4 - Being Age 62 "Throughout the Month"

Social Security has a special rule that applies to retired workers and their wives who file for benefits beginning with age 62. You can not receive a retirement benefit or an aged wife's benefit unless you are 62 throughout the entire month. Generally, this means that you cannot receive a Social Security benefit for the month of your sixty-second birthday, because you are not age 62 throughout that entire month. This rules does not apply to widows.

If your sixty-second birthday is on the first day of the month, you will be eligible because you will be age 62 throughout the month. If your birthday is on the second day of the month, then you are eligible for that month as well, because for Social Security purposes you attain your age the day before your birthday. In other words, if you were born on August 2nd, you become age 62 on August 1st for Social Security purposes. Therefore you are eligible to receive the benefit for that month. If your birthday was on August 3rd, your first month of eligibility would be September. Of course, you can be eligible for benefits for any month after the month you turn 62.

§ 207.5 - The Marriage Requirement

In order to qualify for spouse's benefits or for widow(er)'s benefits, the claimant must have been married to the worker. Generally, this means that the marriage must be recognized as valid in the state where it was performed. A common law marriage will be accepted by Social Security only if entered into in a state which recognizes common law marriages. Most states do not.

A person may meet the marriage requirement even if he or she was not legally married to the worker, if the following conditions are met:
1. There was a marriage ceremony.
2. The claimant married the worker in good faith not knowing any impediment to the marriage.
3. The claimant was living with the worker at the time of his or her entitlement to benefits or at the time of death.
4. There is no other person entitled on the worker's earnings record as a legal wife or widow.
5. The marriage is invalid because there was a legal impediment or there was a defect in the procedure followed in connection with the marriage ceremony. A legal impediment exists, for example, where the worker was already married at the time of this marriage.

This provision is called the "deemed valid marriage." If your benefits are based on a deemed valid marriage, they will end if another person becomes entitled on the account as the legal wife or widow. You may be re-entitled when that other person's entitlement ends.

§ 207.6 - Exceptions to the One-Year Duration of Marriage Requirements for Spouse's Benefits

In most cases, to be eligible as the spouse of a worker, the marriage must have lasted for a least one year before eligibility begins. There are however some exceptions to this general rule. These exceptions are as follows:
1. The claimant is the natural parent of the worker's child. This requirement is met if a live child was born to the worker and the claimant even though the child may not be alive at the time the claimant applies for benefits; or,
2. The claimant was entitled or potentially entitled (under Social Security or Railroad Retirement) to spouse's benefits, widow's benefits, parent's benefits, or childhood disability benefits in the month before the month of marriage to the worker. "Poten-

tially entitled" means that you could have received benefits if you had applied for them. Your age is not considered when determining whether or not you are potentially entitled.

§ 207.7 - Exceptions to the Nine-Month Duration of Marriage Requirement for Widow's Benefits

The general rule is that to be eligible for widow's benefits, you must have been married to the worker for at least nine months before the death of the worker. There are some exceptions to this rule. The exceptions which apply to spouses (see §207.6) also apply to widows, in addition to the following:

1. The worker died because of an accident.
2. The worker's death occurred in the line of duty while he or she was a member of a uniformed service on active duty.
3. The claimant was previously married to the worker and divorced from him and the previous marriage lasted at least nine months.

NOTE: For these three exceptions to apply, the worker must have been expected to live for at least nine months at the time of marriage.

§ 207.8 - The "Child in Care" Requirement

If you are the wife or widow of a covered worker, you may be eligible for benefits at any age if you have a child of the worker in your care. To meet this requirement, the child must be entitled on the same earnings record as the one on which you are making your claim. The child must be under age 16 or disabled. If the child is disabled and over 16, you can be eligible if you are performing personal services for the disabled child.

Please note that the child may continue to receive benefits until age eighteen, but your entitlement will end when the child turns 16 unless he is disabled.

The child does not have to be physically in your custody to meet the "in care" requirement. If you are exercising parental control and responsibility over the upbringing of the child, you may still satisfy the requirement. For instance, if the child is away at boarding school, you may still be eligible if you are reviewing his work and providing parental guidance. Note however, that if you are separated from the other parent of the child you cannot meet the "child in care" requirement while the child is in the custody of the other parent. A child is considered in your care if he is with you at least one day of the month. If, for instance, the child goes to the other parent on July 15th, and comes back to you on August 15th, you will meet the requirement for both July and August. If the child did not come back until September 15th, however, you would not meet the requirement for the month of August. For any month in which the child is not in your care, you are not entitled to benefits and they are suspended. Once the child returns to your care, the benefits may resume.

If the child is over age 16, but is disabled, you may still meet the "in care" requirement if you are performing personal services for the child. Personal services include such things as helping the child wash himself, feeding the child, dressing the child, and so forth. Personal services require that you render more services than for a non-disabled child.

§ 207.9 - The Child Relationship Requirement

In addition to a natural child, certain other kinds of children can be eligible for Social Security benefits. These are adoptive children, stepchildren, equitably adopted children, and grandchildren.

To be eligible, an adopted child must either have been adopted before the worker becomes eligible for benefits or before the child becomes 18. If the child turned 18 and was adopted after the worker becomes entitled, then the child must have received one-half support from the worker and lived with him for the 12-month period preceding the worker's entitlement to benefits. The adoption must be legal.

The stepchild must be dependent on the worker (§207.10) and the marriage of his parent to the worker must have lasted one year (9 months for survivor cases). Note however, if the stepchild is living in the same household as the worker at the time of entitlement to benefits the stepchild is deemed dependent. If the stepchild is entitled, the benefits will not be terminated even if the parents divorce at a later date.

A child may be equitably adopted if there was an intent by the worker to adopt the child but he was unable to complete the legal requirements. If you have a possible case involving equitable adoption, you should consult an attorney.

Grandchildren may be eligible on the grandparents' account, but only if all of the requirements described in §205.4 above are met. Generally, this means that the parents are either deceased or totally disabled at the time the worker (the grandparent) becomes entitled to benefits, becomes disabled, or dies, whichever is earliest.

§ 207.10 - Dependency Requirements: Children and Grandchildren

The natural and adoptive children of a worker are deemed dependent upon him. This means that there is no requirement for proof of dependency. A stepchild who is living with the worker at the time the worker becomes eligible does not have to prove dependency. However, in all other cases there must be proof that the child was dependent on the worker for at least one half of his support in the year before the worker became eligible for benefits or died, in survivor cases.

Basically, Social Security will itemize all the reasonable and necessary expenses for the child's food, clothing, shelter and education and will total these expenses. If the worker was making contributions to the child's support which are equal to or greater than one-half of these living expenses, the dependency requirement will be met.

Chapter 3
Entitlement on More Than One Account

§ 301 - In General

Under certain circumstances, you may be entitled to benefits based upon two separate social security accounts. This chapter explains these situations.

§ 302 - On Your Own Earnings Record and as a Wife

If your Primary Insurance Amount (§702.1) based on your own earnings record is less than one-half of your husband's you may be eligible for additional benefits on your spouse's account. If your husband is actually entitled to a retirement or disability benefit at the time you make your application for benefits (even if benefits are being suspended) you must file for spouse's benefits if your Primary Insurance Amount is less than one-half of your husband's.

Even if you intend to file only for spouse's benefits, you have enough work credits on your own account you will be required by Social Security to file on your own account as well.

The general rules are that you must file on your own account if you have enough quarters of coverage to be fully insured (§602) and you must file on your spouse's account as a wife if your spouse is then entitled to benefits and your Primary Insurance Amount is less than one-half of his. This rule applies even if your husband is not actually receiving monthly benefits because they are being suspended (usually because of earnings). If he is not entitled because he has not yet applied, the rules do not operate because you cannot be eligible as a wife on an account that has not yet been established.

The rule that requires a wife to file on her husband's account even when his monthly benefits are being suspended can result in an unwanted reduction of the wife's benefit. This occurs when the husband is working, but is "entitled" to a retirement benefit which is not being paid because of the excess earnings. Even though no monthly benefit is being paid, he is legally entitled. Let's say the wife is age 62 and has worked on her own account. She applies for a retirement benefit, and her Primary Insurance Account is less than one-half of her husband's. She is required to file on his account as a wife. If she is not working (or is earning less than the allowable limit) she will receive a benefit on her own account reduced for age (§703.1).

Assuming the husband's earnings are high enough that no wife's benefits are payable on the husband's account, the wife's benefit amount will be fixed at the full age reduction for age 62 (§703.1). This means that if the husband stops working in two years when the wife is age 64, she will be paid the wife's benefit in addition to her own, but the amount of the wife's benefit will be reduced 36 months, the same as if she had been receiving it all along, instead of just 12 months, the amount it would be reduced if she was first entitled at exactly age 64. Fortunately, the reduction factor will be readjusted when she becomes 65 (§704.4). However, for the twelve months for which she will receive the wife's benefit before age 65, she will suffer the full reduction.

A person who is entitled to a retirement or disability benefit and to a wife's benefit will receive the regular benefit on her own account, reduced for age if the retirement benefit is taken before 65 plus the difference between one half of the spouse's Primary Insurance Amount and her own. The difference will be reduced for age if taken before 65, with the wife's reduction factor for age figured as of the time of entitlement to the wife's benefit.

Let's look at the situation of Howard and Wanda, who are husband and wife. They are both the same age, have both worked, and are each eligible for retirement benefits. Howard is working full time with substantial earnings. Wanda is not working. They have just turned 62. Wanda applies for her retirement benefit. Her Primary Insurance Amount is $500. Because she is age 62 the Primary Insurance Amount is reduced 36 months (for each month before age 65) and the benefit amount is $400. Two years later Howard retires and files for retirement benefits. His Primary Insurance Amount is $1200. Wanda decides to apply for wife's benefits on his account. Note that she has the option of waiting until she is 65 to file for the wife's benefit. When she applied for her retirement benefit on her own account, her husband was not entitled to the benefits because he had not applied. Nevertheless, she applies now for the wife's benefit. The amount is derived by taking one-half of her husband's Primary Insurance Amount ($1,200 divided by 2 = $600, subtracting her Primary Insurance Amount ($500) and then reducing the difference ($100) by the number of months she is before age 65 at that time, which is 12. Using the wife's reduction factor (§703.1), the $100 difference becomes reduced to $91. In this example then, Wanda receives $400 on her own account plus $91 on her husband's account.

§ 303 - On Your Own Account and to Widow's Benefits

If you are potentially eligible on your own earnings record and on the record of your deceased husband (see Chapter 2 for Eligibility Requirements) you have different options. You may receive benefits on your own account or on your husband's account. If you are under age 65, you may take reduced benefits on one account and switch to unreduced, or less reduced, benefits on the other account at age 65. We will discuss the rules that apply to these situations according to your age.

Under Age 62

If you are under age 62 you cannot receive retirement benefits on your own account. Beginning with age 60 you can receive regular widow's benefits. If you take a widow's benefit before age 62 it will cause a permanent reduction in your own retirement benefit (§703.1). The dollar amount of reduction of the widow's benefit caused by entitlement to the widow's benefit before age 62 will be deducted from your retirement benefit even if you don't receive the retirement benefit until age 65. It will also be deducted from a retirement benefit payable before age 65. However, if the regular age reduction for taking the retirement benefit before age 65 is greater, only the greater reduction is used, not both. Computation of benefit amounts is discussed fully in Chapter 8.

Example: Jane Doe becomes age 60 and applies for widow's benefits. Her husband's Primary Insurance Amount (§702.1) is $1000. The widow's age reduction factor (§703.1) causes a reduction of $285 based on 60 reduction months because Jane is 60 months under age 65. Jane has also worked and earned enough to be entitled to a retirement benefit on her own account. She continues to receive the widow's benefit until she turns 65, and applies for benefits on her own account. Her own benefit would then be reduced by $114 because she received widow's benefits for 24 months before she turned age 62, and the dollar amount of reduction of the widow's benefit caused by entitlement before age 62 is deducted from her own benefit (§703.1). In this case the dollar amount of reduction is 19/40 of 1% (the widow's age reduction factor) times 24 (the number of months for which she received widow's benefits before age 62) times $1,000 (her husband's Primary Insurance Amount) which equals $114. If she had received only 12 months of widow's benefits before age 62 (for example, is she had returned to work for one year and her benefits were suspended because of excess earnings) then the amount of reduction is less, corresponding to the number of months before age 62 for which the widow's benefits were actually paid. If only 12 months of widow's benefits were paid before age 62, the reduction amount would be $57 (19/40 of 1% times 12 times $1,000). Of course, if the widow's reduced benefit is higher than her own benefit, she will continue to receive the widow's benefit amount.

Between Age 62 and Age 65

At age 62 you can receive a retirement benefit on your own account or a widow's benefit on your husband's account. Whichever one you take, it will be reduced for age by the number of months you are under age 65 when you become eligible. See §703.1 for a discussion of reduction of benefits. You can take a reduced benefit on one account before age 65, and then take the other one unreduced at age 65 (unless you have taken a widow's benefit before age 62 as discussed above). Your decision as to which one to take now and which one to take at 65 can only be based on the dollar amount of each benefit, reduced and unreduced. Before making any decision you must obtain benefit estimates (§1403). When you contact Social Security make sure that you file a protective filing statement (§402). When you visit or call your local office, you should deal only with a Claims Representative (§105). It is important to provide him or her with recent earnings information to obtain the most accurate estimates (§1403). The ultimate decision can only be yours. Social Security cannot suggest which decision to make, they can only give you the information upon which to base it.

Example: Jane Doe retires at age 62. She has worked under Social Security and is a widow. She goes to her District Office and learns that her Primary Insurance Amount is $1000 and that her deceased husband's Primary Insurance Amount is $1200. Her benefit reduced for age at 62 would be $800 (§703.1) and her widow's benefit reduced for age at 62 would be $994 (§703.1). She can receive either $800 on her own at 62 and $1,200 on her husband's at 65, or she can receive $994 now on her husband's and $1,000 on her own at 65. What should she do?

In the above example, no one can tell her what to do. She must consider her own particular circumstances, including her current income requirements. A helpful way to analyze the situation is this: Jane can receive an extra $194 per month for the 36 months she will receive benefits before age 65 if she takes the widow's benefit first, but she will get $200 less per month starting at age 65, because the husband's unreduced amount is $1,200 as opposed to her unreduced amount of $1,000. If she does this she will receive a total of $6,984 more ($194 x 36 months) before age 65. If she does not take this higher benefit now and instead decides to wait until 65 to get the extra $200 per month, it will take her 35 months after age 65 to get back the benefits she could have received before age 65. This analysis does not take into account interest the extra money now could be earning, assuming it was invested.

Not counting interest, if Jane should take the widow's benefit at 62 instead of her own benefit, she will start losing money approximately three years after she turns 65. If she took the lower benefits on her own account at 62, it would take her approximately three years after 65 to get back the money she passed up, but after that she would be ahead $200 per month. If her income requirements allow, and if she expects a normal life span, it may very well be to Jane's advantage to take the lower benefit on her own account at 62, and the higher widow's benefit at 65. Of course, if she were on a tight budget, or did not expect to live past 68, she might be better off taking the higher benefit now.

Age 65 and Older

If you are age 65 or older at the time you first become eligible for benefits, you will receive benefits on the account which has the higher benefit amount. See Chapter 7 for a complete discussion of the computation of benefit amounts.

§ 304 - As a Wife and as a Widow

If you are a widow and have remarried, you may be eligible either as a widow or as a wife. Generally, widows who remarry cannot collect widows benefits on their deceased husband's records, unless they have remarried at age 60 or over (age 50 for disabled widows, §904). If you have remarried after you turn 60 and your husband is eligible for retirement or disability benefits, you can receive benefits on whichever account gives you the higher benefit. Usually this reduction for age, is only one-half of the husband's Primary Insurance Amount (§702.1). But in cases where the widow's benefit is less than the wife's benefit, you will receive the higher wife's benefit. Your entitlement as a widow, if you were receiving widow's benefits before you remarried or before your husband became eligible, would terminate upon your entitlement as a wife.

Since January 1984 divorced widows who remarry after age 60 (age 50 for disabled divorced widows) may continue to be eligible for the widow's benefits the same as non-divorced widows.

§ 305 - As a Wife and as an Ex-Wife

If you are divorced from a person receiving Retirement or Disability benefits, you cannot receive benefits as an ex-wife if you have remarried. In these cases you can only receive benefits as the wife of your present husband if he is eligible for Retirement or Disability benefits. You must be married to your new husband for at least one year before you can be eligible, unless you meet one of the exceptions listed in §207.6.

§ 306 - As the Widow of Two or More Workers

If you are the widow of two or more workers, you can receive benefits on the account which would give you the highest benefit. You cannot take one reduced widow's benefit under age 65 and then switch to another widow's benefit unreduced at age 65. Once you have picked which account to take benefits on you cannot later change to a different husband's account.

§ 307 - Disability Benefits and to Retirement Benefits

When a person age 62-64 is entitled to Retirement benefits and is also eligible for Disability benefits, he or she has the choice of taking one or the other of these benefits. If you are age 65 or over, you can take only the Retirement benefit. This is equal to the Disability benefit. But if you are under 65, the Retirement benefit is reduced for age (§703.1). The Disability benefit is not reduced for age, and so it is usually to your advantage to take the Disability benefit. However, if you have two or more eligible dependents, Retirement benefits may be better because the Retirement Family Maximum may be higher than the Disability Family Maximum (§703.2). There is a waiting period during which no Disability benefits are payable. This period is the first five full months of total disability (§507). If you are age 62 or older during one or more of the months of the disability waiting period, you can receive the reduced Retirement benefit during that time. The Retirement benefit will be reduced in the normal fashion depending on your age (§703.1). When your disability waiting period is over, you will then switch over to the Disability benefit. The Disability benefit will be permanently reduced, but only by the number of months you received Retirement benefits before switching to Disability, not by the full amount of the reduction used to figure the Retirement benefit.

Example: John Doe becomes totally disabled beginning with the month he becomes 62. No Disability benefits are payable for the first five months, so he takes reduced Retirement benefits starting with age 62. His Retirement benefit is reduced by 36 months, because he is 36 months under age 65. When his disability waiting period is up he switches over to Disability benefits. Because he received Retirement benefits for only five months before becoming entitled to the Disability benefits, his Disability benefit is reduced by only five months.

§ 308 - Child Entitled on More Than One Account

A child under age 18 or disabled before age 22 (§§205.1-205.4) may be entitled on more than one parent's, step-parent's or grandparent's account. In this case he will be paid on the account which gives the highest benefit.

As discussed in §703.2, when two or more dependents are entitled on one account, the Family Maximum can limit the total amount of benefits payable so that each dependent may suffer a reduction of the benefit amount payable to him. However, when a child is entitled on more than one account, and there are other children entitled on one or more of these accounts, the Family Maximum for each account can be combined so that the reduction of benefits which would otherwise apply can be avoided, and each child can receive the full amount payable.

§ 309 - Other Combinations of Benefits

When a beneficiary is entitled to a combination of different benefits other than what has been discussed in the foregoing sections, the basic rule is that he or she will receive on the benefit which gives the highest monthly amount. If the beneficiary has worked long enough under Social Security to be entitled to a benefit on his or her own account, then a benefit on that account will be paid, even if it is lower, but the difference will be added from the other account.

Chapter 4
Applications

§ 413   Processing Time Frames
§ 414   Withdrawal of Application

§ 401 - In General

To be eligible for Social Security monthly benefits or Medicare, an application must be filed with the Social Security Administration (SSA). SSA has its own forms for applying for the different kinds of benefits and these must be used. It is a policy of most SSA offices not to mail out blank application forms although sometimes they will mail out a blank application form to an attorney. They prefer their own personnel to complete the applications. This does not necessarily mean that you have to make a personal visit to a District Office to file an application. Telephone service is available to file claims (§103). To do that, you will have to give all the information over the phone to a Social Security employee who will fill out the application and then mail it out to you for your review and signature.

The date an application is filed can be very important. It can affect how much you can receive in past-due benefits. You can protect your filing date without having to file an application by filing a "protective filing statement" (§402).

Generally, if you believe that you are entitled to benefits you should file an application. This will require SSA to make a formal decision on your claim, it will protect your rights to any other benefits to which you may be entitled, and it will give you the right to appeal if you are dissatisfied.

Occasionally, a person is told that he cannot file an application because he does not meet some requirement. This is not true - you can always file an application. If you do not meet the requirements the application may be denied, but that does not mean that you cannot file it. If there is any doubt you should file the application to get a formal decision.

§ 402 - The Protective Filing Statement

Any written statement showing an intent to claim benefits filed with the Social Security Administration (SSA) can protect the filing date for an applicant who later files the formal application. In certain cases, this could be very important to prevent a loss of benefits which would otherwise be payable.

As discussed below in §406.1, an application for Retirement benefits may not be retroactive in certain cases. This means you cannot receive benefits for any month before the month you file the application even if you were eligible. If a protective filing statement were filed, it would protect the filing date of an application filed at a later date to allow for the payment of back due benefits. For example, let's say John Smith turned 62 in January but is still working. He files a protective filing statement with his local District Office in January. In March, he is laid off and will have earnings less than the annual earnings limitation (§802.1) so that benefits could be payable starting from January on. If he goes to his local District Office in April and files an application for retirement benefits he can receive past due benefits starting with January, the first month he is 62 because he filed a protective filing statement in January. Let's take the same case except that John Smith did not file a protective filing statement with his local District Office in January. He goes to the Social Security office in April and files an application for benefits. He can receive benefits only for April on. He will lose the benefits for the months of January, February and March. A full discussion of the retroactivity rules for retirement cases is discussed below in §406.1.

In order to qualify as a protective filing statement, the statement must be written, it must indicate an intent to claim benefits and it must be signed by the claimant, the claimant's spouse or by a person who could sign an application (§403). The protective filing statement must be filed with SSA and will protect benefits starting with the month in which it is filed.

SSA considers the protective filing statement filed as of the date it receives it or the date it is mailed by the U.S. Postal Service. In that case, the postmark will be used as the date of filing if that is before it is received by Social Security. Of course, it is a good idea to mail a protective filing statement by certified or registered mail, return receipt requested, so that you can prove the date it was mailed.

SSA will also accept as a date of filing of a protective filing statement the date such a statement is filed with a Medicare-participating hospital in which you are a patient as long as the hospital sends the statement to SSA.

After receiving a protective filing statement SSA will send a notice to the claimant advising him that an application must be filed within six months. The protective filing statement will be effective for that six-month period. The six-month period does not begin however, until

Social Security actually sends the notice. If they never do, then the protective filing statement could be good forever.

If you are eligible to receive benefits and visit your Social Security office to obtain information about benefits, you should file a protective filing statement even if you do not intend to claim benefits immediately. If it turns out a few months later that you could have been eligible when you visited the Social Security office, the protective filing statement could mean additional benefits payable to you.

When filing a protective filing statement, it is a good idea to get a copy. If you visit your District Office and the Claims Representative prepares a written statement for you to sign to protect your filing, ask him for a copy and also ask him to date-stamp your copy so that you can prove that it was filed on that date. Protective filing statements have been known to get lost in the local District Office. As long as you have your copy with a date stamp you will not have to worry about that. Likewise, when mailing a protective filing statement, you should send it by certified or registered mail to prove the date it was mailed and also keep a copy of it.

There is no set format for the protective filing statement but it should contain language similar to the following: "I wish to claim Social Security benefits." The statement should then be signed by the claimant, by the claimant's spouse or by a person who would be able to file an application (§403).

§ 403 - Who May File an Application

The person who claims benefits must sign an application if he or she is 18 years old or over, is mentally competent and physically able to sign. An application for child's benefits may be signed by a parent or a person standing in the place of a parent. A child between the ages of 16 and 18 may sign his own application if he or she is mentally competent, has no court appointed representative and is not in the care of any person.

If the claimant is a minor, is mentally incompetent or physically unable to sign, an application may be signed by a court appointed representative or a person who is responsible for the care of the claimant, including a relative. If the claimant is in the care of an institution, the manager of the institution may sign the application. The Social Security Administration (SSA) has the discretion to accept an application signed by someone other than a claimant if it is necessary to protect the claimant from losing benefits. For example, Mr. Jones becomes bedridden at the end of a month due to a severe medical condition. He asks the neighbor Mr. Smith to go to the Social Security office to file an application for him before the end of the month so that he may receive the benefits for that month. SSA may accept an application signed by Mr. Smith. However, it would be a good idea if Mr. Jones signed a written statement saying, "I wish to claim Social Security benefits" and gave that statement to Mr. Smith to take to the Social Security office. There would be no doubt that such a statement would be a protective filing statement and could protect that month's benefits (§402).

Although persons other than the claimant may file an application under certain conditions, the claimant must be alive when the application is filed in order for it to be effective. There are some exceptions to this general rule.

One, if a disabled person dies before filing an application for disability benefits, a person who would be eligible to receive benefits due to a deceased beneficiary (§1408) may file the application. Although an application for disability benefits may be filed after the worker dies, such an application must be filed within three months after the month of death. For example, John Smith dies in June of 1995. He had been totally disabled for two years before his death but never filed for Social Security benefits. He was married and his wife was living with him. She may file an application for the past due disability benefits as long as she makes the application or files a protective filing statement no later than September, the third month after his death.

The second exception to the rule is if a protective filing statement (§402) was filed by the claimant and he died before an application was filed. In such a case the date of filing is established by the date of the protective filing statement submitted by the claimant and an application may be filed by a person who would be eligible to receive benefits on the deceased's earnings record or by a person acting for the deceased's estate.

§ 404 - When to File an Application

§ 404.1 - In General

An application may be filed before the first month of entitlement. It will be effective until acted upon but no benefits will be payable until the first actual month of eligibility.

As noted in §406.1 through 407 there are different retroactivity rules for different kinds of applications. If an application is filed after the first month in which you are eligible for benefits, the application may or may not have retroactive effect to entitle you to past due benefits. The application should be filed before the retroactive life of the application expires so that you do not lose benefits. For example, in the case of a person who is over 65, an application can be retroactive for up to six months (§406.1). If you become age 65 in March and have no earnings for March or later, you will be eligible for benefits. In order to receive the maximum benefits, you must file the application no later than September. If the application is not filed until October, it can go retroactive for only six months so that the earliest benefits could begin would be April and you would lose the month's benefits for March.

As noted in §407, it is important to file an application before the month you turn 65 even if you do not intend to collect monthly benefits, to avoid losing some Medicare coverage.

§ 404.2 - When to File for Retirement Benefits

The rule of thumb frequently heard is that you should file an application for Retirement Benefits three months before you plan to retire. This is good general advice.

However, there are certain situations where you can actually lose benefits by following this guideline. The earnings test (§801) and retroactivity rules (§406.1) work together in such a way that hundreds or even thousands of dollars may be payable to you even though you are still working.

Depending on the amount of your annual earnings and depending on the amount of your benefit, it is possible to receive some benefits even if you have not retired. An application (or a protective filing statement, see §402) must be filed at the right time, otherwise these benefits could be lost. Let's take the example of John Smith. He will turn 65 in December of 1996, will work throughout the whole year of 1996 and earn total annual earnings of $40,000.00. He goes to the Social Security office to file his application for Medicare coverage in September of 1996. He learns that his unreduced benefit at age 65 will be $1,000.00. The benefit figured for January of 1996 (an 11 month reduction for age - §703.1) would be $938. Based on his annual earnings, the sum of $9493 will have to be withheld from any benefits payable to him in 1996 (§802.2). If his month of entitlement to benefits began with January of 1996, a total amount of $11,256 ($938 x 12) would otherwise be payable for 1996 but only the amount of $9493 would have to be withheld based on his annual earnings leaving the sum of $1763 payable for 1996. However, because he didn't file his application until September, he can go retroactive for only six months to March of 1996 (§406.1). Only benefits for the months of March through December will be payable. Total benefits for these months (10 x $950 = $9500) are only $7 more than the amount that has to be withheld based on his annual earnings. If he files his application in July or earlier in 1996, he will be eligible for the payment of $1,763 for 1996. Although the benefit is reduced for figuring benefits for January through November starting with the month he turns 65 it will be readjusted (§704.4) and he will receive the full unreduced benefit thereafter. When the readjustment occurs an additional $62 will be paid for December to bring the payment up to the unreduced amount (he turns 65 in that month). All future benefits will be unreduced.

Another situation where benefits may be lost even though you file three months before you retire is if your yearly earnings will be less than the annual earnings limitations (§801). For example, let's say Jane Smith will turn 65 in May of 1996, at which time she plans to retire. Her yearly earnings will be less than $11,520, the yearly limit for those turning 65 in 1996. She goes to her local Social Security office in February, three months before she turns 65, and files an application for retirement benefits. She will be entitled to monthly benefits beginning with the month of February, the month she filed her application. Because her annual earnings will be less than the annual earnings limitation, she is potentially eligible for benefits for all months of 1996. However, because payment of the benefit for the month of January would result in a permanent reduction for age, her application cannot be retroactive (§406.1). If she had filed her application in January, she would have been able to receive a benefit for that month. Although this would cause an extra reduction because of age, the reduction would be only a few dollars per month. She would receive hundreds of dollars for the January benefit.

It is impossible to know whether or not you should file an application for benefits before the usual three-month rule of thumb without knowing the exact benefit amount and the exact amount of your yearly earnings. However, if you will earn less than the annual earnings limit (§801) in any year you are at least age 62, you should file a protective filing statement (§402) during the month of January of that year. At the same time, you can request a benefit estimate (§1403) and then make an informed decision as to when you should start your retirement benefits (§408).

If you will be working during the year you turn 65 and earning over the applicable earnings limitation for the year, it would be a good idea to file a protective filing statement in January, but in no case later than July of the year and at the same time obtain a benefit estimate. In this way, if it turns out that you can receive benefits by having a January Month of Election (§408) you will be protected. In 1996, if you turn 65 and have the maximum benefit, you can earn over $55,000 and still receive some benefits for the year. If your spouse is also eligible on your account, some benefits may be payable even if you earn over $75,000. Of course, this all depends on your exact benefit amount and your exact yearly earnings. But to maximize the benefits payable for a year you are working, you should have a January Month of Election. You cannot have this if you do not file an application or protective filing statement before the end of July. A retirement application cannot be retroactive more than six months (§406.1).

If you will have a "non-service" month (§804) at any time after age 62, you should file a protective filing statement no later than the first such month. This is a month where your wages are below the monthly limit, and you do not perform substantial services in self-employment. You may be eligible for a benefit for such a month, despite your annual earnings. In some cases you may not wish to take this benefit (§408), but if you file the protective filing statement, you will preserve your option.

§ 404.3 - When to File for Medicare

Medicare has two parts: Hospital Insurance and Medical Insurance (§§1202 and 1203). An application for Hospital Insurance may be retroactive for six months. However you must file for Medical Insurance before the month you turn 65 (§407) to avoid losing some coverage. Therefore, you should file for Medicare at least one month before you turn 65, even if you are still working.

You now have the option of filing only for Medicare, without having to file for Retirement Benefits. Social Security prefers you to file the retirement application even if you are working, and place your benefits in suspense. Usually this makes no difference, but in some cases it does.

If you have a wife under 65 who will be eligible for benefits on her own account and yours, she may be better off if you file only the Medicare application if you cannot receive benefits. If her benefit is less than one half of yours, she will be required to file for spouse's benefits when she files for her own benefits if you are "entitled" on your retirement account, even if you are in work suspense. If she is under 65, this will cause the amount of her spouse's benefit to be reduced based on her age at that time. If you retire before she turns 65, the extra age reduction for her spouse's benefit stays in effect until she turns 65 (§302).

If you are self-employed, you may be able to exclude some of your income from earnings for purposes of the earnings limitation, but you may require a different month of entitlement for retirement (§408).

If you have a "non-service" month (§804) in the year you turn 65, but do not wish to use it because you will have more non-service months in a later year, you may have to restrict your filing for Medicare only to do this (§408).

Social Security does not usually suggest that you split your entitlement to Medicare from retirement entitlement. It is up to you to specifically request this if it is to your advantage.

§ 404.4 - When to File for Survivor Benefits

As noted in Chapter 2, certain widows, widowers, children and parents of deceased workers may be eligible for monthly benefits. The earliest such an application could be filed, of course, would be the month of death of the covered worker. In the case of Child's Benefits, Mothers' or Fathers' Benefits (these are benefits payable to widows or widowers who have children under 16 or disabled adult children in their care) and in the case of Parents' Benefits, there is no reduction for age. Therefore, an application for these types of benefits may be retroactive up to six months (§406.1). Applications for these types of benefits usually should be filed within six months of the date of death. Of course, an application can be filed at a later date so long as the eligibility requirements are still met but such an application can be retroactive for only six months and benefits may be lost if it is filed later than six months after the death. Sometimes, however, you may wish to start entitlement at a later date (see §408).

In the case of a disabled widow or widower between the ages of 50 and 59, an application can be retroactive for up to twelve months (§406.1). If you became disabled after your husband or wife died, you must file an application no later than 17 months after the beginning of your disability to avoid a loss of any benefits. This is because there is a five-month waiting period before any benefits are payable (§507). If you became disabled before your husband or wife died, then you must file an application within 12 months of the month of death in order to avoid the loss of any possible monthly benefits. This is because the waiting period during which no benefits are payable may be used up during months before the death of your husband or wife.

In the case of benefits payable to widows or widowers age 60 and over, an application cannot be retroactive if it would result in a payment of a full monthly benefit reduced for age (see §406.1). This means that if you file an application for widow's benefits before you are 65, you cannot receive full benefits for any month before the month of filing. (The only exception to this rule is the widow who files for benefits the month after her husband dies. Her application can be retroactive one month to the month of death.) Depending on the amount of your earnings and the amount of the benefit, some benefits may be payable even though you are working (§408). Therefore, it is a good idea to at least file a protective filing statement (§402) in the first month in which you may be eligible for widow's or widower's benefits and then obtain benefit estimates (§1403) to determine whether or not you should file an application. The same principles noted in §408 also apply to widow's claim. You may lose benefits in certain cases if you wait to file until three months before you plan to retire.

If you have worked on your own account and may be eligible for a Retirement Benefit in addition to the Widow's Benefit, you will have an option as to which one to receive (§303).

If you are a widow but were entitled to wife's benefits before your husband died, you may not have to file an application (§405).

§ 404.5 - When to File for Spouse's and Child Benefits

Generally, you should file an application for these types of benefits at the same time as the worker files. Child's Benefits (§§205.1-205.4) and Young Wife's Benefits (§204.2) are not reduced for age, so usually there is no disadvantage to early filing. These applications may be retroactive for up to six months if the worker is retired (§406.2). Applications filed after these periods may result in a loss of benefits.

As noted in §405, a worker should file a protective filing statement (§402) in January of the year he turns 65, even if he is working. If a wife may be eligible on the account, she too should file this statement.

If a person who may be eligible as a spouse files on her own record, she will be required to file as a wife as well, even if no wife's benefits are payable because of the husband's earnings (§302).

See §408 for a discussion of some advantages to starting benefits at a date later than the first possible month of entitlement.

§ 404.6 - When to File for Disability Benefits

An application for disability benefits may be filed any time after a worker stops doing Substantial Gainful Activity (§504). Basically, this means that you cannot file for disability benefits until you stop working. There is a full five-month waiting period before any disability benefits are payable (§507). You may file your application before this waiting period is up, although no benefits will be paid to you until then. It should be noted, however, that for a period of disability to qualify under Social Security, it must be expected to last for 12 months (§502). As noted in §406.2, an application for disability benefits may be retroactive for up to 12 months. To avoid the loss of any monthly benefits, an application for disability benefits should be filed no later than 17 months after the beginning of disability. The first five months of the disability constitute the waiting period. Because the disability application can be retroactive for 12 months, you will not lose any benefits if the disability application is filed within seventeen months after the disability begins.

If your disability has already ended, you may still apply for disability benefits so long as the application is filed within 12 months of the end of your disability (§508). However if you fail to file a disability application because your physical condition limited your activities to such an extent that you could not complete and sign an application, or if you were mentally incompetent, you may file an application for disability within 36 months of the end of the period of disability and still receive some benefits.

§ 405 - When You Don't Have to File an Application

In certain cases where you are already entitled to one kind of benefit, and then become entitled to a different type of benefit, you will be automatically changed over to the new kind of benefit without having to file an application. This is called "automatic conversion" and it occurs in three basic cases. These are as follows:

The first case occurs when you are entitled to Wife's Benefits and your husband dies. If the basis of your entitlement as a wife is because you have a child in your care (§207.8), you do not have to file an application for Mother's Benefits. Mother's Benefits are payable to widows who have children in their care. If you are entitled to Wife's Benefits based on age, you will be converted to Widow's Benefits automatically if you are 65 or older at the time of death of your husband. If you are under 65 without a child in your care, your benefit will be automatically converted to Widow's Benefits only if you are not entitled to a benefit on your own account. This is because the widow has the option of receiving on her own account or on her husband's (§303).

The second situation where you can be automatically converted to a new kind of benefit occurs when you are receiving Disability Insurance Benefits and turn age 65. You do not have to file a new application for Retirement Benefits. There will be no change in your benefit amount. You will simply be converted over to the retirement rolls and taken off the disability rolls. The amount of your Retirement Benefit will be the same as the amount of your Disability Insurance Benefit.

The third situation where automatic conversion occurs is where a child is entitled to benefits as a dependent and the worker dies. The child will be then automatically converted to surviving Child's Benefits and the benefit amount will be increased accordingly.

§ 406 - Retroactivity Rules

§ 406.1 - Retroactivity and Retirement and Survivors

Applications for these benefits (including dependent) can not be more than six months retroactive, and sometimes they may have less or no retroactivity. "Retroactivity" means that you can be entitled to benefits for months before the month of filing. If you file a protective filing statement (§402) your formal application is considered filed in the month the protective filing statement is filed, if that is an earlier month.

Retirement and survivor applications may not be entitled to the full six months retroactivity if the benefits payable before the month of filing are reduced for age (§703.1). If they are not reduced for age, either because you are over 65 or because they are not subject to age reduction, then the application has a full six-month retroactivity.

Benefits reduced for age are Retirement (§202), Aged Wife's (§204.1), and Aged Widow's (§204.4) if they are paid before age 65. Benefits not reduced for age are Young Wife's (§204.2), Mother's (§204.5), Child's (§§205.1-205.4) and Parent's (§206). Applications for Disabled Widow's Benefits (§204.6) may be retroactive for up to twelve months, the same as applications for regular Disability Benefits (§406.2).

Example: Harry turns 65 in January; his wife Wanda is age 63. They both file their applications in July. Neither Harry or Wanda has earnings over the applicable limits (§801). Harry's benefits can begin with January because this is no more than six months before the month of filing and the retroactive benefits are not reduced for age because his is 65. Wanda's benefits cannot start before July, the month of filing, because the retroactive benefits would be reduced for age (§703.1). Note that if she had filed a protective filing statement (§402) in January her benefits could begin as of January even though the application was not filed until July.

Exception 1

An application for Retirement Benefits may be retroactive for up to six months even if the worker's benefits would be reduced for age if there is a dependent entitled on the account who could receive unreduced benefits retroactively, such as a wife over 65, or a child.

Example: Harry turns 64 in January, and his wife Wanda is then age 65. They both file in July. Wanda has never worked and files as a wife on Harry's account. Harry's earnings are under the limit for the year. Both applications may be retroactive six months to January. Although Harry's benefits are reduced for age, Wanda's wife's benefits are not because she is 65. Because Wanda is entitled to Harry's account, Harry's application may be retroactive as well.

Exception 2

Another exception which allows retroactivety for a Retirement or Survivor's application where the retroactive benefits are reduced for age, occurs when the claimant has excess earnings for the year (§801) and the retroactive months are used to satisfy the earnings test (§803). The application may be retroactive for as many months during the calendar year of filing as are required to be charged against excess earnings, but not more than six. The retroactivity cannot go into the past year. The reason for filing retroactively is to allow for the payment of some benefits before you stop working.

Example: John will be age 65 as of November, 1996. He will retire at the end of August and have total yearly earnings of $25,000, with no work for September on. He visits his District Office in July. He learns that his Primary Insurance Amount (§702.1) is $900. His benefits as of September, reduced for age (§708.1), would be $889. He therefore expects to receive $3,556 in benefits for 1996 ($889 per month for September through December). The earnings limits for those 65 in 1996 is $11,520 (§802.2). One dollar in benefits must be withheld for every three dollars earned over this limit (§802.2). Therefore $4,493 [($25,000-11,520) divided by 3] must be withheld from John's 1996 benefits, except for months he has no earnings (§804). Because he is working through August, he expects that his benefits should begin with September. But John can get additional benefits for 1996. John has filed in July. If his benefits before the month of filing are charged against his excess earnings, his application can be retroactive up to six months, to January. If John's Month of Election (§408) is January, the benefit amount with the additional age reduction (§703.1) would be $849.

Based on $25,000.00 earnings, $4,493 must be withheld from benefits. If benefit eligibility starts in January at $849, benefits for the months of January through June would be withheld (January through May in full and part of June) to satisfy the withholding requirement. A partial payment of $601 would be payable for June, and $849 for July on, even though John is still working. At age 65, the reduction factor will be adjusted to eliminate the reduction caused by entitlement for the months of January through June, because benefits for these months were not paid in full (§704.4). Because benefits before the month of filing are charged against earnings, John's application can be retroactive up to six months. Note that June's benefit is considered to be charged against earnings even though a partial payment for this month is due. As long as a part of the benefit is withheld, it is considered to be charged against earnings.

If John's earnings were less so that his excess earnings would be charged to less than six months of benefits, the retroactivity of the application would be reduced to only the number of months required to charge excess earnings. In the example above, if his earnings were only $18,000.00, only $2,160 would be chargeable against benefits. Only three months of benefits (two full and one partial) would be used to offset excess earnings and the retroactivity of the application would be limited to three months.

Exception 3

If one of the months in the retroactive period is a "non-service" month (§804) i.e. a month where earnings are under the monthly limit, the application may still be retroactive even though a reduced benefit is payable for that month, provided that the non-service month is not the first month of entitlement, and provided that all other months before the month of filing are used to offset excess earnings.

Example: Jim turns 62 in January. He has $45,000.00 yearly earnings in 1996, but had no earnings in February. He will retire in August and files for benefits in July. His application may be retroactive six months to January. The benefits for January, and March through July must be withheld because his excess earnings are high, but February's benefit is payable because it is a non-service month (§804). If he had filed in August, he could not receive the February benefit because it would be the first month of entitlement. The application cannot be more than six months retroactive, so January could not be the first month, as it is seven months before August.

Wives and Widows

Wife's Benefits are subject to withholding due to the worker's earnings (§803), but even so, her application for Wife's Benefits cannot be retroactive if she is under 65 unless her own earnings would require offset against her monthly benefits. If she has no earnings, her application cannot be retroactive if she is under 65 even if her husband's can be. Of course, is she is entitled as a wife because she has a child in her care (§204.2), her application may be fully retroactive (six months) because this type of Wife's Benefit is not reduced for age.

Aged Widow's Benefits (§204.4) are reduced for age if taken before age 65 (§703.1) and therefore applications may not be retroactive if benefits would be reduced for past months. An exception is for the widow who files in the month after the month of the worker's death. The application may be retroactive only one month. If the application is filed in the second or later month after the month of death, it may not be retroactive. Of course, if the widow's earnings require offset against benefits, the application may be retroactive in the same way as applications for Retirement Benefits.

§ 406.2 - Retroactivity and Disability

An application for Disability Insurance Benefits or Disabled Widow's Benefits can be retroactive for up to 12 months. This means if you were otherwise eligible for disability benefits within the 12 months before the month you file your application, you may be paid for them. You may not be paid for months before the 12 month period before the month you file your application. For example, you become disabled on January 11, 1995. No benefits are paid for the first five *full* months of disability (§507), so that for February through June, no benefits will be payable (January does not count because it is not a full month of disability). Beginning with July of 1995, benefits could be payable. Assume you did not apply for disability until September of 1996. Because the application can be retroactive for only 12 months, the first month for which you can receive disability benefits would be September of 1995. When your claim is approved, the first payment will include payment for September, 1995 to date. You will lose the benefits for July and August, 1995.

Applications for Child's or Wife's Benefits on the account of a wage earner who is entitled to Disability Insurance Benefits are also entitled to the twelve-month retroactivity, with the exception of Aged Wife's Benefits (§204.1), if the wife is under 65. In this case, the rules in §406.1 apply to her. If you were disabled in the past but have recovered and returned to work, you may still apply for the disability benefits for the past months you were disabled (§508) but only for those months within the 12 months of the date you file your applications. There is an exception to the 12 month retroactivity rule for applying for a *period of disability*. If you were mentally incompetent or your physical condition limited your activities so that you could not complete and sign an application, you may file for a period of disability within 36 months of the end of the disability. Although no benefits can be paid more than 12 months retroactively, if a period of disability is established, a "freeze" (§503) can be placed on your earnings record.

§ 407 - Rules on Medicare Enrollment

To be eligible for Medicare coverage, you must be 65 or have been disabled and receiving social security benefits (including Disabled Widow's and Disabled Adult Children) for 24 months. This is in addition to the full five-month waiting period. In other words, at the time you receive your 25th Social Security disability check, you will be eligible for Medicare coverage. Medicare coverage is also available for those who are on kidney dialysis (see Chapter 12).

As noted in Chapter 12, Medicare has two parts, Hospital Insurance and Medical Insurance. These have been referred to in the past as Part A (Hospital Insurance) and Part B (Medical Insurance), although Social Security no longer officially uses these letters to designate the different parts of Medicare because they can cause confusion with beneficiary identification codes (§1407).

You may apply for Hospital Insurance at any time after you are eligible. An application for this part of Medicare coverage can be retroactive for no more than six months. If you are receiving monthly benefits when you first become eligible you will be enrolled automatically.

The rules are very different when it comes to Medical Insurance. This part of Medicare covers doctors bills (§1203).

You must apply for it *before* your first month of eligibility to be covered at the earliest time. Medical Insurance is optional. You must pay a premium for it even if you are entitled to regular monthly benefits. If you are receiving benefits at the time you become eligible, you will be notified a few months before that Social Security will automatically enroll you in Medical Insurance and will start deducting the premiums from your benefit checks. If you are not entitled to monthly benefits at the time you turn 65, you must make the application for Medical Insurance yourself.

If you apply for Medical Insurance (also called supplementary medical insurance) *before* the month you turn 65, coverage will begin on the first day of the month in which you turn 65. If you apply for Medical Insurance *during* the month you turn 65, it will become effective on the first day of the *following* month.

If you apply the *month after* you turn 65, your coverage will begin the *third month* after you are 65. Filing the *second month* after 65 grants you coverage starting the *fifth month* after you are 65. Filing in the *third month* covers you starting in the *sixth month* after your 65th birthday.

If you do not apply for Medical Insurance within three months after the month you turn 65, then you are limited as to when you can apply for it and when it can begin. The period of time around your 65th birthday including the month of your 65th birthday, the four months before your 65th birthday and three months after your 65th birthday are referred to as the "Initial Enrollment Period." If you do not apply for Medical Insurance during that time, then you can only apply during the first calendar quarter of any year thereafter. This is the "General Enrollment Period." That would be January, February, March of a following calendar year. If you miss your Initial Enrollment Period and then you apply for the Medical Insurance during a General Enrollment Period, Medical Insurance coverage will not become effective until July 1st of that year. Additionally, if you have gone 12 months or more without having Medical Insurance coverage after the month you first could have been eligible, the premium that you pay for Medical Insurance will be increased (§1203).

If you did not enroll in Part B (Medical Insurance) because you were covered by an employer group health plan (see §1204), you are entitled to a "Special Enrollment Period." This is a seven month period beginning with the first month your group coverage ends. You may enroll in Part B during this time. If you enroll in the first month, your Part B coverage begins with the first day of that month. You should do this to avoid a gap in coverage. If you enroll in a later month of the Special Enrollment Period, your coverage begins with the first day of the *next* month. If your group coverage ends before the end of a month, that month will be considered the first month of your Special Enrollment Period *if* you sign up for Part B during that same month. In this way you will not have any gap in coverage. Otherwise the first month will be the *next* month (the first full month you are not covered by the group plan).

You are also entitled to a Special Enrollment Period near the time you turn 70, because your employer is not required to cover you after age 70. The Special Enrollment Period for this begins with the third month before the month you turn 70 and lasts seven months. If you enroll during one of the first three months, your Part B coverage begins with the month you turn 70. If you enroll in the month you turn 70 or a later month, coverage begins the first day of the month *after* the month you enroll. To avoid any gap in coverage, you must enroll *before* the month you turn 70. Note that Social Security considers you to turn 70 the day before your 70th birthday. This is important if your birthday is on the first day of the month. If you lose group coverage in the month you turn 70 or earlier, the rules stated in the first two paragraphs of this section will apply if that will give you coverage earlier.

To be eligible for the Special Enrollment Period, you must be covered *both* by Hospital Insurance (Part A) *and* the group plan in at least one month. If you are not already covered by Part A you must apply for it. The application may be retroactive for no more than six months. For this reason, if you don't have Part A, you *must* file *before* the seventh month of the Special Enrollment Period.

You are limited to one Special Enrollment Period if you did not enroll in Part B when you were first eligible for it (i.e., during your Initial Enrollment Period). If you did enroll then, but later cancelled, you may have more than one Special Enrollment Period only if you were covered by both Part A and a group plan when you cancelled Part B. Additionally, you must enroll in Part B during a Special Enrollment Period each time you lose group coverage.

These rules also apply if you have group coverage based on your spouse's employment, regardless of your spouse's age.

Even if you do not plan to retire, you should contact your local Social Security Office before the month you turn 65 so that you can apply for Medicare without losing any coverage or having to pay any additional premiums.

§ 408 - When to Start Your Benefits - The Month of Election

As noted in §§406.1 and 406.2 above, applications for monthly benefits may, in certain circumstances, be retroactive. This means that you may start your legal entitlement beginning in a month before the month you file your application. If you are filing for a type of benefit which is not reduced for age, such as Young Wife's Benefits (§204.2) or Mother's Benefits (§204.5), then there is no disadvantage to beginning your legal entitlement at the earliest possible time with some exceptions discussed below. However, if you are applying for a benefit which may be reduced for age and you are under 65, you may have to make a choice. For example, Retirement Benefits and Widow's Benefits paid before 65 are reduced for age (§703.1). As a result, if your entitlement to benefits begins earlier than the month you apply for benefits, it will be reduced by a larger amount because of the age reduction. You will be younger when the entitlement begins so that the benefit will be reduced more. However, sometimes the additional benefits you gain by going retroactive as far as possible can offset the amount of the extra reduction so that you may be better off by starting your benefit at an earlier date. For Retirement or Widow's Benefits, the month you choose your legal entitlement to benefits to begin is called "The Month of Election."

Let's take the example of John. He will be 65 in September of 1996. He plans to work through the month of August 1996 and his total 1996 earnings will be $27,000. He will retire beginning with September. He goes to his local District Office in June to make his application. He is informed that his Primary Insurance Amount is $900.00. The Primary Insurance Amount is the unreduced benefit amount that is payable at 65. Because John will be working and earning money through the month of August and he will turn 65 in September, he assumes that the month his entitlement to benefits should begin is September. However, it will be to his disadvantage to start his benefits as of September. It works like this:

His 1996 earnings will be $27,000. By applying the Work Test (§802.2), we find that the amount of $5160 must be withheld from benefits payable for months in which John will earn over $960 (a full discussion of the Work Test is found in Chapter 8). This means that the months of January through August are subject to withholding of benefits. If John's Month of Election is January, his $900.00 Primary Insurance Amount is reduced to a benefit amount of $859 per month because he is eight months under age 65 as of January. Applying the Work Test, we know that the sum of $5,160 must be withheld from benefits. But for the months of January through August, the total benefits at $859 per month for those eight months is $6,872. This leaves $1,712 in benefits payable for this period.

The monthly benefit of $859 per month will be withheld in full from January through June and the sum of $6.00 will be withheld from the July benefit, leaving $853 payable for July. The benefit amount of $859 for the month of August is payable so that he will receive total benefits of $1712 for July and August (a partial benefit of $853 for July and a full benefit of $859 for August). An application for Retirement Benefits can be retroactive for up to six months if you are under 65 if benefits payable before the month of filing are charged against excess earnings (§406.1). This is the case with John. The benefits payable for January through June and part of July's benefit are actually payable before the month he applies, therefore he can start his legal entitlement to benefits with January. By doing so, he will use up the amount of benefits that will have to be withheld ($5,160) before he stops working. By doing this, a benefit for the month of August and a partial benefit for the month of July in the total amount of $1,712 can be paid

John turns 65 in September and his benefit will be adjusted to take out any reduction for a month before 65 in which he did not receive a full monthly benefit (§704.4). In John's case, he received a full monthly benefit before 65 only for the month of August. The month of July does not count because part of the benefit for that month was used to satisfy the Work Test. Therefore, at 65 the reduction months will change from eight reduction months used to figure his benefits as of January to only one permanent reduction month for the month of August. Because of this readjustment, as of September his benefit will be reduced by only one month so that the benefit amount will be $894. Although he suffers a permanent reduction in the amount of $6.00 per month, he has received $1,712 in benefits before 65. Instead of doing this, if John started his legal entitlement with the month of September, the month he turned 65, he would receive no benefits for the period of January through August and receive $900.00 per month starting with September.

Although he would get $6.00 more per month, he would not have the $1,712 which he would get with a January Month of Election. If John passed up the opportunity to get his additional $1,712 in benefits before

65 it would take him twenty-three years to get that money back, without figuring interest! Clearly it is to John's advantage to start his legal entitlement as of January instead of September even through it means a small permanent reduction in his monthly benefit. Note that John must file his application no later than July, because an application for Retirement Benefits cannot be more than six months retroactive in any event. Of course, if John had filed a Protective Filing Statement (§402) before July, it would protect his filing date for this purpose.

These principles also apply to Widow's Benefits which may be reduced for age.

As a general rule, especially in the year you become 65, it is to your advantage to start your month of entitlement as early in the year as possible. Of course, it all depends on your Primary Insurance Amount, your expected yearly earnings, and your age. The factors you should consider when deciding whether to start your legal entitlement with the earliest possible month or a later month are how much in benefits you can receive before the later month, and how much extra reduction for age that will cause. You should also note that the adjustment of the reduction factor occurs at 65 so that if you take an extra reduction for age, the monthly benefit amount will not be changed to eliminate months which are not payable because of earnings until you turn 65. If you take a reduced benefit at age 62, that reduced benefit amount will stay in effect until you turn 65.

Sometimes you may be better off with a later month of entitlement. If you are self-employed you should consider a special rule which excludes self-employment income from earnings for purposes of the retirement test (§808). Self-employment income received after your first *year* of entitlement, but attributable to services before the *month* of entitlement will not be included.

For example, Jim is a self-employed plumber who turns 65 in July 1996. He expects $30,000 net earnings in 1996, and $30,000 net earnings in 1997. $7,500 of his expected 1997 earnings will result from services rendered in 1996 but before December 1996. When he files for Medicare, he learns that based on his expected 1996 earnings and his benefit amount, he could receive $600.00 in benefits for 1996 with a January 1996 month of election, and without suffering any permanent reduction in his benefit. However, because of the special exclusion rule, he will be better off with a December 1996 month of election, even though he loses the $600.00. With a December 1996 month of election he can exclude the $7,500 he expects to receive in 1997 from that year's countable earnings because it is attributable to services rendered before December 1996, his month of entitlement, and received after the first year of entitlement. This means his 1997 countable earnings will be only $22,500. Under the 1 for 3 rule (§801) he will receive $2,500.00 more in 1997 benefits than if his countable income were $30,000. When he files for Medicare in 1996 he will have to limit his application for Medicare only (§404.3).

If your earnings are high enough to prevent payment of benefits, but you are eligible for a "non-service" month (§804), you may wish to forego this benefit if you will have more non-service months in a later year and wish to use them then. Generally you are eligible for non-service months in only one year. For example, Bill is a merchant who earns $60,000.00 a year and does not plan to retire. However in 1996 he will not work in July and may be eligible for benefits for that month.

In 1997 he will have the same annual earnings, but will not work in February, July or August. Clearly he is better off if he receives benefits for the three non-service months in 1997, rather than only one in 1996. To do this, his first month of entitlement must be later than July 1996. If he is eligible for Medicare earlier, he may restrict his filing for Medicare only (§404.3).

At one time, you could not change the Month of Election that you chose at the time you filed your application unless you withdrew the application. Now, the Month of Election is conditional and can be changed at a later date so long as the new Month of Election is within the retroactive life of the application (§406.1).

You will require the assistance of a Claims Representative to figure out what your best Month of Election should be in close cases. When you visit your District Office to discuss this, make sure that you have as accurate an estimate of annual earnings as possible. Also make sure that you file a Protective Filing Statement (§402) with your District Office no later than July (preferably in January) of the year in which you turn 65 so that you may take advantage of a January Month of Election if that would result in extra benefits payable to you. If you go to your District Office to get a benefit estimate (§1403) and to discuss this question, make sure that your last two year's earnings are included (bring your W-2 forms or tax returns) and that your estimated earnings are as accurate as possible.

For a complete discussion of the choices that a widow who is entitled to a Widow's Benefit as well as a benefit on her own account must make, see §303.

§ 409 - Required Documents

§ 409.1 - In General

You need different documents depending on what type of claim you file. These will be discussed in the following sections in more detail. Social Security always requires original documents. You cannot make a photocopy of a birth certificate or W-2 form. It will not be accepted by Social Security without the original.

Sometimes clerks of Vital Statistics Offices will give you a photocopy birth certificate. If this is the case, make sure that the photocopy has an original raised seal or is stamped and signed by the clerk. This is what is referred to as an original copy.

When you bring your documents into Social Security, they will make their own photocopies and return the documents to you. As noted above, however, you cannot give them the photocopies in the first instance; they must see the actual original documents.

Sometimes people delay filing a claim for benefits because they do not have all of their required documents together. This could be a very bad mistake which could result in the loss of benefits. Do not wait to gather all of your documents together before filing your claim. Although it is a good idea to have the documents on hand when you file, it is not a good idea to delay filing. You can file an application and submit the documents at a later time when you get them. Sometimes Social Security will get them for you. It is important that your application be filed at the earliest possible time so that you may receive all the benefits to which you are entitled. If you are late in filing the application, you may lose benefits. Of course, if you have your documents together when you file your claim, this will speed the processing, but you should note that the processing of the claim can begin even without all the documents. Try to get your documents together well before you intend to file your claim, but when it comes time to file don't delay even if you don't have them all.

§ 409.2 - Required Documents for Filing
a Retirement Claim

When you file a claim for Retirement Benefits, you will need your birth certificate or other acceptable proof of age (§410). You will also need all W-2 forms for the last two years. The W-2 forms are the statements of earnings issued by each employer and show the total amount of your annual earnings. The reason you need these documents is that Social Security's records of earnings are behind by at least one year and sometimes two years. These W-2 forms will establish your earnings so that they can be used in figuring your benefit. Please note that if you had more than one employer, you should make sure you bring W-2's from each one. Also, some people receive W-2 forms from a union or some other source of earnings. Make sure you bring these as well.

If you are self-employed, you will need the last two or three years' income tax returns for yourself as well as for your business (§412).

§ 409.3 - Required Documents for Filing a Wife's Claim

When you file a wife's or husband's claim, whether because you are 62 or because you have children in your care, Social Security will require your birth certificate. However, a marriage certificate is not required. Instead, Social Security will require your husband or wife to sign a form which certifies that you are presently married.

Note that if you are filing an application on your own earnings record as well, you should bring your last two year's W-2 forms if you have worked within the last two years (§409.2).

If you are filing as a divorced wife (§204.3) you will need your marriage certificate and final divorce decree.

§ 409.4 - Required Documents for Filing a Widow's Claim

When you file a claim for Widow's Benefits, you will need your husband's death certificate, your own birth certificate and your marriage certificate. If you are filing as a Surviving Divorced Wife, you will also need your divorce papers. Additionally, if your husband had worked within the last two years, you will need his W-2 forms from all his employers.

Note that if you were receiving Wife's Benefits you may not have to file a new application (§405).

§ 409.5 - Required Documents for Filing a Child's or Parent's Claim

When filing a child's claim you will need a birth certificate for each child. If the child is a stepchild, the marriage certificate of the natural parent to the worker will also be required to establish the relationship. For adopted children, the adoption papers will be required. For illegitimate children, it will have to be proven that the father acknowledged the child as his own before he became entitled to Social Security benefits or before he died. The proof can take the form of signing a report card as the father or signing for the hospital bill at the time of the birth of the child or other such documents. Any written acknowledgment will suffice.

In the case of a person filing as a grandchild, there must be proof of death (a death certificate) or disability of both parents as well as birth certificates of the grandchild and the parents to establish the relationship to the worker. Disability will not be something you can get in a document. You must supply names and addresses of treating doctors and hospitals. Social Security will obtain the records.

§ 409.6 - Required Documents for Filing a Disability Claim

We do not discuss medical evidence or medical requirements in this section, only documents which must be produced at the time the application is filed. For a person who is filing for disability benefits on his or her own account, a birth certificate will be required if you are born in the year 1930 or later or if you are age 59 1/2 or older at the time the application is made. Proof of age if you were born in 1930 or later is required because there is a special insured status requirement for persons who turn age 22 after 1951. It is the Social Security Administration's policy to obtain a birth certificate for persons who are 59 1/2 or older at the time of the application so that they can be changed over to the Retirement Benefits at age 65 without having to re-contact the beneficiary for proof at that time. You should note that Social Security will not require you to submit any documents in connection with the disability claim until such time as your claim is allowed on the medical evidence. Most disability cases are denied. Therefore, Social Security does not go out of its way to get documents or to require you to get documents until the claim is allowed on medical grounds. Of course, if you have the documents you should submit them when you file because if they are in the file, Social Security can pay you benefits as soon as the claim is allowed. Otherwise, they may have to contact you again after the claim is allowed to obtain the necessary documents.

§ 410 - Proof of Age Rules

Most Social Security beneficiaries receive benefits on the basis of their age. The Social Security Administration (SSA) has very precise guidelines and requirements for proof of age. SSA will not accept just anything.

SSA classifies different kinds of proof of age into two basic categories: Primary Evidence and Secondary Evidence. SSA considers Primary Evidence of age to be either a birth certificate or a baptismal certificate recorded before the age of five.

Usually a birth certificate or a baptismal certificate will contain not only the date of your birth but will also show the date that the document was first recorded. Sometimes a birth certificate is not recorded until years after a person's birth. If your birth or baptismal certificate was not recorded within five years of birth, it will not be accepted as Primary Evidence. Please note that you do not need both a baptismal and birth certificate, either one will do. If you do not happen to have a birth certificate or a baptismal certificate with you at the time you file your application, SSA will not accept other evidence of your age unless there is a satisfactory explanation of why there is no Primary Evidence.

If you were not baptized, obviously you cannot be expected to have a baptismal certificate. However, if you claim that there is no birth certificate for you, SSA may require a statement to that effect from the State Bureau of Vital Statistics. Some states did not record births years ago and SSA has a list of all states which shows whether or not they recorded births. If the state in which you were born did not record births at the time you were born, that will be satisfactory evidence of the unavailability of a birth certificate. However, if your state did record births at the time you were born, SSA generally will require some proof that there is no birth certificate. Such proof would be a statement from the Bureau of Vital Statistics of your state that they searched for your birth certificate and could not find one.

If there is no Primary Evidence as discussed above, then SSA will consider what is referred to as "Secondary Evidence." Secondary Evidence includes such things as a birth certificate or baptismal certificate recorded more than five years after birth and passports, census records, marriage certificates which show your age, immigration records, and so forth (see Appendix 1 for a listing of types of Secondary Evidence Social Security will consider). Additionally, when you applied for your social security number you were asked to give your date of birth and Social Security still has that information. If you submit one piece of Secondary Evidence listed in Section I-1 through I-9 of the list at Appendix 1 and it agrees with the date of birth you gave when you applied for a social security card, no further evidence will be required. However, if you submit two or more pieces of evidence which contain different dates of birth or if there is any discrepancy between the date of birth you gave when you filed for your social security number, and any Secondary Evidence, then SSA will require full development of Secondary Evidence. In this event, they will attempt to get as much as possible of the evidence listed in Appendix 1 and then they can make a determination to establish your date of birth.

When considering the different kinds of Secondary Evidence, they will generally consider as best that evidence which is oldest and which is least likely to be subject to error. For instance, a birth certificate recorded at age seven would be considered very good Secondary Evidence because it was recorded early in life and for a purpose which generally would require that exact date of birth. Date of birth on a marriage certificate or an employment record generally is not considered very good evidence because usually it is recorded later in life and the purpose for which it is recorded doesn't require the exact date of birth. If there is a piece of evidence which shows your date of birth as being younger, such as an employment record or your date of birth on the social security number, you will be asked to explain why it is different. Many people gave a different date of birth when they applied for a social security number. Perhaps the employer took the social security number application form and they wanted the employer to think they were younger. If you did something like that do not be afraid to tell it to Social Security. They will not hold it against you. They are only looking to resolve the discrepancies in the evidence.

§ 411 - Proof of Marriage Rules

To establish your marriage when this is required to be entitled to benefits, Social Security may require your marriage certificate. Of course, marriages are usually recorded and there must be an explanation if you cannot obtain one. You will usually be required to produce a statement from the Bureau of Vital Statistics to the effect that a search was made for your marriage and that no record was found. If there is no record of your marriage, you may establish it by Secondary Evidence. The oldest and best evidence is recorded for a purpose which would require information about marriage, such as a passport or a child's birth certificate which shows the names of the parents. Statements from your husband's relatives may also be obtained. See §207.5 for a discussion of the marriage requirement.

§ 412 - Special Problems for Business Owners

If you own your own business, whether you are self-employed or whether you have set it up as a corporation, you encounter special problems when you claim Retirement Benefits from Social Security. Of course, if you are closing up your business altogether or you are selling it to a third party who is not related to you and you will have no further involvement in the business, you should not have a problem. However, Social Security almost always requires a face-to-face interview if you own your own business. You cannot usually file a claim over the phone. The reason for this is that Social Security wants to question you in detail about your business and determine how credible you appear. The interviewer will make a written determination about whether or not he believes you are telling the truth.

If you are not selling your business outright to a non-relative or you are not closing up shop altogether but you are claiming Retirement Benefits based on a decrease in earnings, you will have to give a complete and thorough explanation as to why your earnings are decreasing. It is not enough to simply cut your salary down on the books. That means absolutely nothing to Social Security. They will want to know what duties you are performing now that you are claiming partial retirement. They will want to see whether or not the earnings that you report are consistent with the duties you perform. They will want to know who is performing the other duties that you are no longer doing and what qualifications they have for this. It is not enough to say simply "My wife will run the business," if she has never been involved in the operation of the business.

If you tell Social Security that you will not go to work on certain days, you can be sure that they will send somebody to your place of business on those days to confirm that you are not there. A Social Security representative may pose as a customer.

You will also be asked to give names and addresses of your major customers and suppliers, because Social Security will contact them to verify that you are no longer dealing with them or that your business is off.

Social Security will require your own personal tax returns for the last two or three years as well as the business tax returns. They will want to see whether or not you are taking income from the business and calling it something other than earnings. For instance, if your business is in the corporate form and your salary is cut but your dividends from the business increase, they will look to see why that is. You may be disguising salary as dividends. They will also look at your deductions to see if any of them are being overstated to hide income. When you make your initial application, Social Security will take a very detailed statement from you as to the operation and management of your company. Be prepared when you make your application to give a full and complete explanation and to thoroughly explain why your earnings will be less than they were before.

§ 413 - Processing Time

In general, it takes about two weeks for an application to be processed to payment. At times it can take as little as one week. Unfortunately, in rare cases it can take months and some cases can take four or five months. Delays can occur if there is a problem with proof of your age or some other requirement, such as marriage. If your first check doesn't arrive within three months of the time you gave Social Security all the information and documents required, you may have a right to what is called an "expedited payment" (§1013). You should note, however, that the checks will not be paid until they are due. If you file early, you will not receive your first check until after the month for which the first payment is due.

As noted in §1003, checks are paid in arrears. This means that, for instance, the July check is paid on August 3rd. The check you receive on the third day of the month is payment for the prior month. If your first month of eligibility will be September and you have made your application in June, you will not receive your first check until October 3rd. If your first month of eligibility is September and you made your application in September, you should expect your first check no later than 90 days after you submitted the last evidence that has been required.

The reason that some cases can be processed to payment within two weeks or so while others take two or three months is that Social Security has a special computer system which can allow the personnel in the local District Office to make the computer entries to pay the case. Not all cases can fit within this computer system, however, and some cases require approval in a Program Service Center (§102). This usually adds to the processing time.

§ 414 - Withdrawal of Application

You can withdraw an application you have filed at any time before a determination is made on the application. If the Social Security Administration (SSA) has already made a determination on the application, it can only be withdrawn if any other person who would lose benefits because of the withdrawal consents to it in writing and all benefits which have already been paid on the application are returned to SSA. If SSA approves a request to withdraw an application, it will be treated as though it were never filed.

A request for a withdrawal of an application must be in writing and filed at the Social Security District Office. The usual case where someone wants to withdraw an application occurs when he has applied for reduced Retirement Benefits before 65. He later resumes working or earns more than he anticipated so no benefits are payable due to the amount of his annual earnings. In that case, it would be to his advantage to withdraw the application so that the reduction for age would be eliminated in the event that benefits later became payable before 65. Of course, at 65 your benefit will be re-figured to exclude the reduction factor for any months for which you did not receive a full monthly benefit (§704.4).

You may also wish to withdraw an application if you use a "non-service" (§804) month in one year, but may be eligible for more non-service months in a later year (see §408).

Eligibility for Medicare coverage is not affected by withdrawal of an application.

Chapter 5
Disability Benefits:
Special Provisions

§ 501 - In General

There are three different kinds of Social Security benefits which are paid on account of disability. The most common and well known is the Disability Insurance Benefit (DIB) (§203). This is the benefit paid to disabled workers. The amount of the benefit is the same as if you were 65. To be eligible for the DIB you must be specially insured (§604). You must have not only worked long enough under Social Security, but you must have worked in the recent past.

The other Social Security benefits paid on account of disability are Disabled Adult Child (DAC) Benefits (§205.3) and Disabled Widow Benefits (DWB) (§204.6). These benefits are paid to children of retired, disabled or deceased workers, and to widows age 50 to 59. See Chapter 2 for the eligibility requirements.

This chapter will not discuss all the aspects of proving a claim for disability benefits because they are too numerous and complicated. An entire book would be required to cover everything. We will discuss the medical requirement only in general terms. If you should file a claim for disability and be denied, you should retain an attorney to represent you (see Chapter 13).

We will discuss in detail those special rules which are unique to disability benefits, other than the medical requirements.

§ 502 - Definition of Disability

As noted in the section above, this book cannot go into a detailed discussion of all the medical requirements for disability benefits. In this section we will discuss only very generally the medical requirements. If you believe you are disabled, you should file an application for benefits. If you are denied after your first application you should consult an attorney. Many cases which are denied are awarded on appeal. The rules regarding the medical requirements are very complex and you should have a lawyer represent you if you appeal. See Chapter 13.

There are three kinds of disability benefits: Disability Insurance Benefits (DIB) (for disabled workers), Disabled Adult Child (DAC) benefits (for children of retired, disabled or deceased workers who become disabled before age 22), and Disabled Widow Benefits (DWB) (for widows between ages 50 and 59 who are disabled). See Chapter 2 for the exact eligibility requirements for these different kinds of benefits.

For disabled workers and disabled adult children, the law defines disability as the inability to do any kind of substantial gainful activity (§504) for a continuous period of at least one year or to result in death. The cause of disability can be either mental or physical, but it must be medically determinable. This means there must be a medical basis for the condition. Statutory blindness also is considered a disability. Statutory blindness is defined as central visual acuity of 20/200 or less in the better eye with the use of glasses, or the field of vision limited so that the widest diameter subtends an angle no greater than 20 degrees. The one year duration requirement also applies to blindness cases.

For disabled widows, the definition of disability is now the same as just stated. Before 1991 the law had a different and stricter requirement. A disabled widow must have been unable to do *any* gainful activity. Note that for the worker or child the requirement is in the inability to do *substantial* gainful activity. As a result of this difference in definition of disability, it was much harder to qualify as a disabled widow. The one year duration requirement (or expected death) also applies in widow's cases.

SSA will consider your age, education and work experience along with your medical condition. This means that even if your medical condition does not prevent all type of work, you may still be eligible if your particular situation, considering age, education and work background, is such that you cannot be expected to perform the only work you are physically able to do. The simplest example of this is the laborer in his late fifties who has a back condition which prevents him from performing his regular job. He has done only this type of work. Although he may still have the physical ability to do light work, SSA will consider him disabled because of his age and limited work background.

To repeat: the rules on proving disability are very complex. If you are unable to do your regular work you should file a disability application. If your claim is denied, consult an attorney and consider an appeal. Many cases which have been denied the first time have been won on appeal.

§ 503 - The Earnings Record "Freeze"

When you are entitled to Disability Insurance Benefits (DIB) you are also entitled to what is called a "freeze" because of its effect on your earnings record. The months or years during which you are entitled to a period of disability will not be considered for purposes of calculating benefits. For instance, if you were disabled for five years during your fifties, when you reach retirement age and apply for Retirement Benefits, the five years of disability will be excluded. This is important because Retirement Benefits are based on your average earnings over many years. If these years of disability were considered, your average earnings would be much lower because you had no earnings during the disability.

Whenever you are eligible for Disability Insurance Benefits, a "freeze" is placed on your earnings record for that period. This happens even if no disability benefits are actually paid, so long as you meet all the requirements. Of course, it is very rare that you would be eligible without being actually paid. When we say "eligible" in this section, we mean being officially determined eligible after making an application, as opposed to being potentially eligible. The usual situation where someone is eligible for a period of disability but no benefits are paid is when the disability is based on blindness and the beneficiary is engaging in Substantial Gainful Activity (SGA). See §504.1 below for this special case.

The disability freeze applies to the computation of all benefits, not just retirement. It also applies when determining the number of quarters of coverage required (§601).

§ 504 - Substantial Gainful Activity

Regardless of your medical condition, if you have done work during a time you claim disability benefits, you will not be eligible if the work is determined to be Substantial Gainful Activity (SGA), unless you are in a trial work period (§509) or it is an unsuccessful work attempt (§506). If you are an employee, rather than self-employed, the most important factor in determining whether the work is Substantial Gainful Activity is the amount of your earnings. SSA has established dollar amounts of earnings to use as guidelines. If the earnings average below $300 per month, the work is not considered SGA. If they average above $500 per month, the work is considered SGA. If the earnings are in between the levels, then additional factors are considered.

Please note that these amounts have increased over time. The above figures have been in effect since 1990 and are still used as of 1996. If the average monthly earnings for the period of work activity are less than $300, the work is not considered SGA and you will be eligible for Disability Insurance Benefits or Disabled Adult Child Benefits. If the earnings average more than $500.00, you will be considered engaging in SGA. You will not be eligible for benefits, no matter what your medical condition may be (Note: see §509 - Trial Work Period and §506 - Unsuccessful Work Attempt).

When SSA considers your earnings for purposes of determining whether or not you are doing SGA, they will disregard any part of your pay which is not based on your actual services. For example you may be working for an employer who is subsidizing part of your pay, as in the case of some sheltered workshops. The employer may be paying more than your work performance is worth economically. The amount of any such subsidy will be deducted from your earnings for the purpose of using the earnings guides discussed above. If the employer does not set a specific amount for such a subsidy, SSA will investigate the circumstances to determine how much of your pay you actually earn and how much represents a subsidy.

Likewise, SSA will deduct from the amount of your earnings any unusual work-related expenses. These expenses, to be deducted, must be incurred because of your impairment and only if they exceed normal work-related expenses. They will not be deducted if you require them even if you are not working, such as expenses for medication.

If your average earnings, after any allowable deductions as discussed above, are in between the high and the low monetary guidelines, SSA will compare your work activity to the work activities of non-disabled people in your community. If unimpaired people are doing the same kind of work as a means of livelihood, your work will be considered SGA. If your work activity is not comparable to the work activity of non-disabled people in your community who are doing it as a livelihood, your work will not be considered SGA. When making these comparisons, SSA will take into account the time, energy, skill and responsibility involved in the work.

If you are self-employed, SSA will not consider the income you earn as the test of whether you are engaging in SGA. Your earnings could be affected by any number of factors other than your disability. If your work activity, considering the time devoted to the business, the skills required, duties, responsibilities, efficiency and energy output is comparable to the work activity of non-disabled people in your community, the work will be considered SGA. If not, then SSA will look to the value of your services to the business. If the value of your services is clearly equal to the high monetary guidelines (currently $300.00 per month) for employees discussed above, the work will be considered SGA. When deciding the value of your services, SSA will look to how much you would have to pay an employee to perform them. If the value of your services is worth less than the high monetary guideline for an employee, then SSA will consider the income you get and whether you render significant services to the business.

If you render significant services and the income you derive is equal to or higher than the high monetary guideline for an employee discussed above, (even if the value of your services is worth less), the work will be considered SGA. If the income is less than this guideline, but the livelihood you earn is comparable to what you earned before you became disabled, or is comparable to what non-disabled self-employed people in your community derive as a means of livelihood, it will be considered SGA. Your services to the business are considered significant if you are the sole proprietor, or if you contribute more than half of the management time to the business, or if you spend more than 45 hours a month on management time, even if that is less than half of the total management time.

§ 504.1 - Substantial Gainful Activity - Special Rules for the Blind

If your disability is based on blindness (see §502) you will be eligible for monthly benefits even if you are working as long as your monthly earnings do not average more than the monthly earnings limit for retired workers age 65 and older (see Appendix 6).

If you have shown an ability to earn amounts equal to the above, your disability benefits will be terminated. However, if you are age 55 or over your benefits will not be terminated if your present work is not comparable to the work you did before you became blind. If your new work requires skills and abilities less than or different from those you used before, your benefits will only be suspended for months in which you have earnings over those listed above. The difference between termination of benefits and suspension is discussed in Chapter 10. If your benefits are only suspended, then you can have them started again without re-applying, and without meeting the one-year duration of disability requirement (§502).

If you meet the eligibility requirements for disability based on blindness (§502) including the work requirement (§604), you are eligible for a period of disability, called a "freeze" (§503), even if you are performing Substantial Gainful Activity. Although no monthly benefits are paid while you are working or able to work, you are entitled to the advantage of the earnings record freeze. You must file an application for this and meet all the requirements as if you were applying for monthly benefits.

§ 505 - The Date of Onset

The date your disability begins is very important. This date determines how your benefit is computed (§702.2) and is used to determine how much work you need and when (§604). It determines when the waiting period (§507) begins and whether or not you can receive retroactive benefits (§406.2).

Your waiting period begins with the first full month of your disability. If you become disabled on the first day of a month, that month will be the first month of the waiting period. If you become disabled on the second or later day of a month, then the *next* month will be the first month of the waiting period. For example, if you become disabled on June 10, your waiting period begins with July. If you become disabled on June 1, June is the first month of the waiting period.

The earlier your date of onset, the better it is for your. Your waiting period will be used up that much sooner so that benefits can start with an earlier month. If your onset is an earlier year, you may require less work credits, or quarters of coverage (§604), and your benefit amount will usually be slightly higher. And the further back you can go for retroactive benefits (§406.2), the more money can be paid for past due benefits when your claim is awarded.

The date of onset is determined by the date your disability actually began, regardless of whether or not your salary continued. For example, if you became disabled on June 10, but your salary was paid until December 20, your date of onset is June 10, not December 20, as long as you actually stopped working in June. If your medical condition started before you stopped working, the time you stopped working is used, not when the condition started. When we say "work" in this section, we mean Substantial Gainful Activity (§504). If you are disabled and return to work, and then stop again because of the disability, the date of onset will be the second time you stopped work, unless your return to work can be considered an unsuccessful work attempt (§506). For example, you become disabled for the first time as of January. You are out of work for the entire month of January, but return to your job on February 15 and work until June 15, when you again stop work, this time for good. Unless the work period from February to June is considered an unsuccessful work attempt (§506), your date of onset will be July. If the work period from February to June is determined to be an unsuccessful work attempt, your date of onset is January.

If you are out of work for an entire year before returning, you may be entitled to a closed period of disability (§508).

§ 506 - The "Unsuccessful Work Attempt"

As noted in §504.1 above, the date of onset of your disability is very important. The earlier your onset, the better it is for you. People who have stopped working because of a disability but have then returned to work before stopping work again may be able to use the earlier date as the date of onset. For example, if you become disabled and don't work at all in the month of January, but then return to work in February and work until April 15, when you finally stop working, you may be able to establish January as your date of onset.

A period when you return to work may be considered an unsuccessful work attempt if it lasts less than three months and you are forced to stop work again because of the physical or mental conditions imposed by your disability. You must still meet the medical requirements of disability as of the first time you stopped working. The first period of disability must have lasted a full month or longer, and there can not have been any medical improvement during the time you went back to work.

A period of work can still be considered unsuccessful if it lasted longer than three months as long as all the conditions discussed above are present and, in addition, the work period does not last more than six months and there are special considerations given by the employer. The work performance for the six months must be less than is required of non-disabled workers.

You may have more than one unsuccessful work attempt, as long as there is at least one full month of disability between them and there has been no medical improvement.

§ 507 - The Waiting Period

There are no benefits payable to either the disabled worker or to any of his dependents for the first five full months of disability. No benefits are payable during the waiting period nor will benefits be payable later for any months within the waiting period. The waiting period begins with the first full month of disability after the date of onset (§506). No waiting period is required if you were previously entitled to disability benefits within five years of your current disability. The waiting period is the first five full months of a period of disability. If you become disabled on the second or later day of the month, that month will not count towards determining your period of disability. For example, if you become disabled on April 15, the first full month of disability will be May, and the waiting period will start counting with the month of May, so that May, June, July, August and September will be the months chargeable to the waiting period and no benefits will be payable for those months. The first month of entitlement to a monthly benefit in that case would be October. The month you become eligible for the payment of the monthly benefits is called your date of entitlement.

The waiting period is only used to determine when the monthly benefits should begin. You must still meet the one year duration requirement mentioned in §502, unless the disability is expected to result in death. You do not have to wait until the end of the waiting period before filing an application for disability. You may file for disability benefits at any time after you stop working due to disability. If you file for disability benefits before your waiting period is up, no benefits will be paid until the waiting period has passed. If it appears from the nature of your disability that it will be permanent or will exceed one year, then it is a good idea to file the application as soon as you stop working because the application will take usually two to three months to be processed and approved. If the waiting period has passed during the time the application is being processed, your benefit checks could begin right away.

For example, you become disabled on April 15, and it appears that your disability will be permanent. The waiting period will be the first five full months of disability, namely May, June, July, August and September. If you apply for your disability benefits during your waiting period, let's say in June, and it takes three months (until September) for the application to be approved, you will get your first disability check as soon as it is payable. The month of entitlement would be October and you would receive your check on November 3, for October. (Checks are paid in arrears - §1003).

If you wait for the waiting period to pass before your make your application, remember that the processing time usually takes up to three months. You would be without benefits during the processing time. Of course, if the claim is approved, the first payment will include any past due benefits payable after the waiting period. In the example just discussed, if you waited to apply until November and it took three months, until February, for the claim to be approved, you would be without your benefit payments for those months, but when the first check comes, it will include payment for October, November, December and January (§1002).

§ 508 - The Closed Period of Disability

As noted in §502, you may be eligible for a disability benefit if your disability lasts for at least one year. An application for disability benefits may be retroactive for up to one year (§406.2). If you have been disabled for at least one year, but then have returned to work, you may be eligible for disability benefits for the period of disability even if you didn't file for the disability benefits at the time. This past period during which you were disabled is referred to as a "closed period" of disability.

You will be eligible for the payment of benefits only for months within the twelve-month retroactive life of a disability application (§406.2).

For example, you become disabled on April 15, 1993, and you recover on June 15, 1994. You return to work at your regular job. You do not file an application for disability benefits until February of 1995. The waiting period (§507) starts running from the first full month of disability, which would be May. It runs from May through September. Your first possible month of entitlement to a disability benefit would be October 1993, and your last month of possible entitlement to a disability benefit would be August 1994 (§513). However, because you did not apply until February 1995, your application can be retroactive for only twelve months, which brings it back to February 1994. Because at the time you apply you have recovered from your disability, the period of time that you were disabled is referred to as a closed period of disability. If the claim is approved, you will be paid retroactive benefits for the months of February 1994 through August 1994. If you had applied for the benefits no later than October 1994, you would have received the benefits for all the months which would be payable, namely from October 1993 (the first month of entitlement) through August 1994.

§ 509 - The Trial Work Period

After you have become entitled to disability benefits you may attempt to work without having your disability benefits immediately terminated if you are still medically disabled. This is referred to as a trial work period. It is different from the unsuccessful work attempt discussed in §506. The trial work period only applies after you have become entitled to disability benefits, but the unsuccessful work attempt applies to work periods before you apply.

The purpose of the trial work period is to allow a disabled beneficiary who is still physically disabled to try to work without penalizing him. Earnings during a trial period have no effect on benefits, even if they exceed the earnings limited which apply to other kinds of benefits. The Work Test (§801) does not apply to disability benefits.

You are not eligible for a trial work period if you have made a medical recovery from your disability or if your medical condition has changed to the extent that you are no longer totally disabled, even if you are partially disabled. You must still meet all the medical requirements of total disability to be eligible for a trial work period.

If you are, then your work, even if it is Substantial Gainful Activity (§504 above), will not be considered in determining whether or not your benefits should be cut off. Of course if the work activity you are performing is not Substantial Gainful Activity, then your benefits will continue. Only months in which you have earnings more than $200 will count towards the trial work period.

You are allowed a total of nine months for the work period. After this your work activity will be evidence that you are no longer disabled.

The nine months of the trial work period do not necessarily have to be consecutive. If you use up two months of the trial work period, stop working altogether for a while, then work for another two months, you will have used up four months of the trial work period and will only have five months remaining. For example, you become entitled to disability benefits in January 1994. In December 1994, you obtain part time employment and earn $100.00 per month from December 1994 until March 1995. This work activity is below the earnings guidelines described in §504 and therefore does not constitute Substantial Gainful Activity. It has no effect on your disability benefits but it does use up four of your trial work period months because it is over $75.00 per month.

However, in April 1995 you begin earnings $600.00 per month. This is Substantial Gainful Activity because it exceeds the earnings guidelines of §504. You continue earning $600.00 per month from April 1995 through June 1995. You have now used up seven months of your trial work period. You stop working in June and have no earnings until September 1995, at which time you again begin earning $600.00 per month, and you continue earning at that rate from then on. Your trial work period months are December 1994 through June 1995 and September and October 1995. That is nine months. Please note that to be eligible for the trial work period, your medical condition must still constitute a total disability. If your medical condition had improved, you would not be entitled to the trial work period.

If you continue working and earning above the Substantial Gainful Activity guidelines (§504) after the expiration of your trial work period, then your work activity would mean that you are no longer disabled regardless of your medical condition. Accordingly, your disability would cease with the first month of Substantial Gainful Activity (§504) after the trial work period expires. You receive an additional two checks after the month that your disability is determined to have ceased (§513).

§ 510 - The Reentitlement Period

The reentitlement period is an additional 36 month period after nine months of trial work during which you may continue to test your ability to work if you continue to have a disabling impairment. You will be paid benefits for months during this period in which you do not perform substantial gainful activity, but you will not receive benefits for any month after the first three in this period during which you perform such work. If anyone else is receiving monthly benefits based on your earnings record, that individual will not be paid benefits for any month for which you cannot be paid benefits during the reentitlement period. If your benefits are stopped because you do substantial gainful activity they may be started again without a new application and a new determination of disability if you discontinue doing substantial gainful activity during this period. In determining, for reentitlement benefit purposes, whether you do substantial gainful activity in a month, SSA considers only your work or earnings for that month; they do not consider the average amount of your work or earnings over a period of months.

§ 511 - The Effect of Workers' Compensation Benefits

If you receive Social Security disability benefits and also receive Workers' Compensation benefits due to an on-the-job disability, your Social Security benefits may be affected.

If the combination of Social Security benefits (including benefits for your wife and children) plus the amount of the Workers' Compensation benefits you receive per month is greater than 80% of your Average Current Earnings (ACE), then your Social Security benefits will be reduced so that the total will come down to the 80% level. Benefits payable to dependents will be reduced first. For example let's say that your Social Security disability benefit is $500.00 and that you have a child under age 18 who is entitled to $250.00. You are also eligible for Workers' Compensation benefits in the amount of $450.00 per month. The total of these benefits is $1,200.00. Let's say that your Average Current Earnings before your disability were $1,000.00 per month. 80% of this is $800.00 per month. Because the combination of the Social Security benefits and the Workers' Compensation benefits is $1,200.00 and 80% of the Average Current Earnings is $800.00, the difference, $400.00, must be subtracted from your Social Security benefits. This $400.00 would be deducted as follows: The dependent's benefit of $250.00 would be entirely eliminated and $150.00 would be taken from your disability benefits.

When determining the Average Current Earnings, Social Security considers the gross amount of your prior earnings, not your net amount after deductions. The Average Current Earnings are figured three different ways. Whichever way will give you the highest average is used.

The *first method* of figuring the Average Current Earnings (ACE) is to take the average monthly earnings during any *one* calendar year within the year of your onset of disability or the five preceding years.

The *second method* of determining the Average Current Earnings is to take the average monthly earnings in any *five* consecutive calendar years after 1950. Note that the five years must be consecutive. You cannot pick any five after 1950; they must follow one after another.

The *third method* of determining Average Current Earnings is to take the average monthly earnings of *all* years used in computing the disability benefit (See §702.2).

Whichever of the three methods produces the highest average per month will be used. It is important to note that for purposes of determining Average Current Earnings, your actual earnings are used even if they exceed the amount of earnings subject to FICA tax for that year. Because your earnings record only shows the earnings in a calendar year which are subject to the FICA tax, it is important if your yearly earnings for a particular year exceeded the FICA maximums to bring this to the attention of the Social Security Administration. For example, the maximum earnings subject to FICA in 1994 was $60,600. Even if you earned over that amount only the FICA amount usually will be recorded on your earnings record. If you earned, for example, $70,000 in that year, for purposes of determining your Average Current Earnings, the $70,000 figure would be used, not the amount shown on your earnings record. A listing of the FICA maximum for all years is located at Appendix 3.

The Workers' Compensation offset does not apply if the Workers' Compensation Law under which you are receiving Workers' Compensation benefits provides that *compensation* benefits will be reduced by the amount of Social Security benefits you receive.

If the total of the Social Security benefits payable on the individual's earning's record is greater than 80% of the Average Current Earnings, then this higher figure is used to figure the offset instead of the 80% figure. For example, if the Average Current Earnings are $1,000.00 per month, 80% is $800.00. If the total amount of benefits payable on the account, including the dependents, is $900.00 per month, then the Social Security benefits will be reduced so that the combination of Workers' Compensation and Social Security benefits do not exceed $900.00. It is rare, however, that the total Social Security benefits exceed 80% of Average Current Earnings.

§ 512 - The Effect of Other Kinds of Benefits or Payments

Benefits paid under private disability insurance policies have no effect on Social Security disability benefits. Employee salary continuation will not have any effect, nor will any back pay, retroactive increases past due, commissions or any other such payments from an employer. Besides Workers' Compensation discussed in §511 above, the only type of disability benefits which affect your Social Security disability are those which are required by any federal, state or local law. For example, some states have laws which require employers to pay disability benefits to disabled employees. Such benefits would be used to offset Social Security disability benefits in the same way as Workers' Compensation. These benefits are added to the amount of Workers' Compensation and the computation of the offset is then the same. You should note, however, that if the statute requiring the special disability benefit provides for an offset for Social Security benefits, then this offset provision does not apply.

§ 513 - When the Disability Benefits End

There is a difference between "cessation" of disability and "termination" of disability benefits. Cessation of disability occurs when Social Security determines you are no longer totally disabled within the definition of disability for Social Security purposes (§502). Termination of benefits occurs two months after cessation of disability. For example, if Social Security determines that your disability ceased in June, your disability will terminate as of August so that you will receive the benefits for June, July and August, but not thereafter.

Cessation of disability occurs when your medical condition is no longer considered to be totally disabling or when you begin performing Substantial Gainful Activity (§504).

Social Security conducts periodic reviews of many Social Security disability cases to reconsider the medical condition of the beneficiary. If, after such a medical review, Social Security determines that your condition is no longer totally disabling, your disability will be considered to have ceased. It is the policy of the Social Security Administration to send you a notice of this determination and if they fail to do so, your disability will not be considered to have ceased until such time as you receive the notice. For example, let's say the Social Security Administration conducts a medical review of your case and determines that based on your medical records, your disability ceased as of June 19, 1984. However, due to office problems, they did not mail out the notice to you until August 1984. It is the Social Security Administration's policy to make your official cessation of disability in August, the month you received the notice, rather than June, the month that they determined your medical evidence no longer was considered totally disabling.

Even if your medical condition remains the same or worsens, if you are performing Substantial Gainful Activity (§504), your disability will be considered to have ceased. Note that if you are entitled to a trial work period (§509) your work activity will not be considered Substantial Gainful Activity until nine months of the trial work period have passed. You may then be entitled to further benefits for non-work months. See §510. Also note that not all work activity is considered Substantial Gainful Activity (§504).

§ 514 - The Continuing Disability Review

The Social Security Administration conducts periodic reviews of disability cases to determine whether or not you are working or whether or not your medical condition has changed. Some cases are reviewed more frequently than others and some cases are not reviewed at all. It depends on the nature of your disability. When your claim is first awarded a date is usually set at that time for a future review.

You will be notified when your case is being called for review and generally you will be called to the District Office to give current information about any work activity you may be doing, to obtain the names of your current doctors and any recent periods of hospitalization. The Social Security Administration may have you examined by one of their consultant physicians, at their expense.

If you do not cooperate with this continuing disability review, Social Security has the authority to stop your disability benefits because you fail to cooperate.

Chapter 6
Insured Status:
The Work Requirement

§ 601 - The Work Requirement in General

To qualify for a Social Security benefit, either you or the person on whose earnings record you claim benefits must have worked a certain amount of time in employment covered by Social Security. Almost all employment in the U.S. is now covered. The work requirement is called "insured status."

There are different kinds of insured status depending on the type of benefits being claimed. "Fully insured" status (§602) is required for most benefits. "Currently insured" status (§603) is required for Young Widows (§204.5) and surviving children (§§205.1-205.4). A special "disability insured" status (§604) is required for Disability Insurance Benefits (§203).

Dependents and survivors are eligible based on relationship to an insured worker. There is no work requirement for them. The person on whose account benefits are claimed must meet the applicable insured status requirement.

The eligibility requirements for the different kinds of benefits are listed in §§202-207.2. Each listing states the insured status requirement for the particular benefit.

The insured status requirement does not affect the amount of the benefit. It sets a minimum work requirement which must be met before any benefit is payable. Once this minimum is met a benefit amount is computed based on average earnings (see Chapter 7).

If you have insured status on your own and also qualify as a dependent or survivor, you may be entitled on both accounts (see Chapter 3).

Insured status is gained by earning Quarters of Coverage (§605.1). These are calendar quarters for which credit now is given based on certain minimum earnings during the year.

§ 602 - Fully Insured Status

Fully insured status is required for most benefits. To be fully insured you must earn one Quarter of Coverage (§605.1) for every year after 1951 up to and including the year you attain age 62 (for Retirement Benefits), become disabled (for Disability Insurance Benefits) or die (for Survivor Benefits). Note that there is an additional requirement for Disability Insurance Benefits (see §604), and that certain Survivor Benefits do not require fully insured status (see §603). For Survivor and Disability Benefits the rule is different if the worker was born after January 1, 1930. Instead of 1951, use the year of attainment of age 22.

Social Security rules provide that you attain your age on the day before your 62nd birthday. For example, if your birthday is on January 1, 1995, you become 62 on December 30, 1994. Therefore, if your birthday is January 1, you attain age 22 or 62 in the year before that birthday for purposes of figuring the insured status requirement.

To collect wife's, widow's or child's benefits you do not have to meet the work requirement yourself. Instead, you must be the wife, widow or child of a worker who meets the requirement.

The minimum number of Quarters of Coverage required in any case is six. The maximum is forty.

To compute the quarters required for Retirement Benefits, subtract 1951 from the year you become 62. For Survivor or Disability benefits use the year of death or onset of disability (§506) instead of the year you turn 62 if this is earlier, and the year of attainment of age 22 instead of 1951 if this is later.

A chart is located in Appendix 2 which lists the quarters required for fully insured status depending on year of attainment of age 62, disability, or death. It applies to those born on or before January 1, 1930.

Here is an example of how the above rules work for someone born after that date: John was born August 11, 1950. He became disabled on June 5, 1994. We add 22 to the year of birth (22+1950=1972). John attained age 22 in 1972. We subtract 1962 from the year of onset of disability (1994-1972=22). John needs 22 Quarters of Coverage (§605.1) to meet the fully insured part of "disability insured" status (§604).

§ 603 - Currently Insured Status

This type of insured status requires less Quarters of Coverage (§605.1) than fully insured status (§602). However, only some kinds of benefits can be based on currently insured status. These are Surviving Child's Benefits (§§205.1-205.4), Mother's Benefits (§208 - also called Young Widow's Benefits') the Lump Sum Death Benefit (§207.2), and Medicare for kidney failure cases (§207.3).

A worker must earn at least six Quarters of Coverage (§605.1) within the thirteen calendar quarter period ending with the calendar quarter of death. The calendar quarters are as follows: first quarter - January, February, March; second quarter - April, May, June; third quarter - July, August, September; fourth quarter - October, November, December.

To determine this period, take the quarter and year of death, subtract three from the year; the period begins with the quarter of the resulting year which corresponds to the quarter of death. For example, Jim died on May 15, 1995. This is in the second quarter of 1995. We subtract 3 from 1995, which equals 1992. The thirteen quarter period begins with the second quarter of 1992 and ends with the second quarter of 1995. If Jim earned six Quarters of Coverage (§605.1) during that period, including the beginning and ending quarters, he is currently insured.

§ 604 - Disability Insured Status

Eligibility for Disability Insurance Benefits (§203) requires a special "disability insured" status. You must be fully insured (§602) and meet a second requirement of recent Quarters of Coverage (§605.1). This second requirement is different depending on when you become disabled.

If you become disabled in or after the calendar quarter you reach age 31, you must have at least twenty Quarters of Coverage (§605) during the 40 calendar quarter period ending with the quarter your disability begins (see §505). To determine this period, subtract 10 from the year the disability begins and begin with the first quarter after the quarter in the resulting year which corresponds to the quarter of onset of disability. The calendar quarters are as follows: first quarter - January, February, March; second quarter - April, May, June; third quarter - July, August, September; fourth quarter - October, November, December.

For example, John becomes disabled on September 5, 1994. This is the third quarter of 1994. Subtracting 10 from the year bring us to 1984. The corresponding quarter of that year is the third quarter. The 40-quarter period begins with the first quarter after the corresponding quarter. Therefore the period begins with the fourth quarter of 1984 and ends with the third quarter of 1994. If John has 20 Quarters of Coverage within this period, including the beginning and ending quarters, he will meet the second part of the "disability insured" status requirement.

Sometimes the requirement is referred to as the "five year" rule or the "five year out of ten year" rule. This is somewhat misleading. Although 20 quarters is five years and 40 quarters is ten years, the legal requirement is based on quarters, not years. The 20 quarters required do not have to be consecutive, they can be spread out. The 40-quarter period does not always correspond to the beginning and ending of calendar years. This rule is more accurately called the 20/40 rule, i.e. 20 quarters required in the 40-quarter period.

If you become disabled before the calendar quarter of your 31st birthday, there is an alternative to the 20/40 rule. Instead, you must have one Quarter of Coverage (§605.1) for every two calendar quarters in the period beginning with the calendar quarter after the quarter of your 21st birthday and ending with the quarter of onset of disability (see §505). If the number of quarters in this period is an odd number, use the next lower even number. A minimum of six quarters of coverage is always required. Quarters of Coverage earned before age 21 may be used if this is required to meet the requirement.

If you were disabled before age 31 and received benefits based on the alternative to the 20/40 rule just discussed, but then your disability ceased and you become disabled again after age 31, you will meet the disability insured status requirement even if you cannot satisfy the 20/40 rule if you have at least one Quarter of Coverage for every two calendar quarters beginning with the quarter after attainment of age 21 and ending with the quarter of the new onset date. You exclude any quarter wholly or partially within the prior period of disability, except the beginning or ending quarters if they are Quarters of Coverage.

In all cases, you must be fully insured (§602).

§ 605 - Quarters of Coverage

§ 605.1 - Quarters of Coverage in General

A Quarter of Coverage is a calendar quarter for which credit is given by Social Security for purposes of deciding if a person has worked long enough to qualify for benefits (see §601). A minimum amount of wages from covered employment or self-employment income must be earned to get credit. Almost all employment and self-employment is now covered by Social Security. The amount of earnings required to get credit has changed. The rules are discussed in the following sections of this chapter.

§ 605.2 - Quarters of Coverage - Pre 1978 for Employees

In years before 1978, you receive a Quarter of Coverage for each calendar quarter during which you were paid $50.00 or more. It doesn't matter when the wages were earned. The Quarter of Coverage is assigned to the quarter in which the wages were paid to you. However, if you were paid maximum yearly earnings subject to Social Security, (the FICA maximum), you are given credit for the four quarters of that year, even if the earnings were paid in less than four quarters. The yearly FICA maximums are listed at Appendix 3.

There is a special rule which applies to farm workers for years before 1978. Instead of the $50.00 per quarter rule, a farm worker received one Quarter of Coverage for each $100.00 in cash wages paid during a year, without regard to the quarter in which the wages were paid. Quarters of Coverage were assigned beginning with the last calendar quarter and then counting backward.

Beginning with 1978, the rules for all employees have been changed (§605.3). The rules have always been different for the self-employed (§605.4).

§ 605.3 - Quarters of Coverage - Post 1977 for Employees

Beginning with 1978, Quarters of Coverage are assigned based on total yearly earnings instead of earnings paid within a calendar quarter. A certain amount has been designated for each year and one Quarter of Coverage is credited for each multiple of that amount which is paid within the year. These amounts are listed in Appendix 2, Chart 1.

Example: John was paid $800.00 in 1984, when the required multiple was $390. He is credited with two Quarters of Coverage because his earnings are at least two multiples of $390.00, but less than three multiples. Jim was paid $1,600.00 in 1984. He receives four Quarters of Coverage because his earnings are at least four multiples of $390.00.

No more than four Quarters of Coverage are given for one calendar year. A Quarter of Coverage cannot be assigned for any quarter which has not yet started, nor for any quarter which begins after the worker's death.

§ 605.4 - Quarters of Coverage for the Self-Employed

The method of determining Quarters of Coverage for self-employed individuals is different than it is for employees. Before 1978 the self-employed person received four Quarters of Coverage for a year if the net earnings from self-employment were $400.00 or more. If the net earnings from self-employment were less, the self-employed did not receive any Quarters of Coverage. It was all or nothing. Beginning in 1978, the rules changed. For 1978 and all later years, a self-employed person receives Quarters of Coverage based on the amount of total yearly earnings in the same way as an employee (§605.3). However, the self-employed individual must still meet a minimum of $400.00 in net earnings from self-employment to receive *any* Quarters of Coverage.

For example, John works as a plumber for the Smith Plumbing Company. He earned $350.00 in 1978 in wages. He receives one Quarter of Coverage, because this is more than the minimum required earnings for one Quarter of Coverage as discussed in §605.3. Joe however, is a self-employed plumber. His net earnings from self-employment in 1978 were $375.00. He receives no Quarters of Coverage even though his net earnings from self-employment are greater than the minimum earnings required for an employee. If he earned $400.00 in self-employment income in 1978, he would receive one Quarter of Coverage. If he had earned $400.00 in net earnings from self-employment in 1977, he would have received four Quarters of Coverage.

If you are both self-employed and an employee, add your total earnings as an employee and your net earnings from self-employment to determine how many Quarters of Coverage you will receive using the rule described in §605.3. However, to count *any* net earnings from self-employment into the yearly total they must be at least $400.00. If the net earnings are less, they are not added in at all. For example, Joe is both self-employed as a plumber and works as an occasional employee of Smith Plumbing Company. In 1978 he had $400.00 in net earnings from self-employment and $350.00 in wages. Combining the two sums equals $750.00. Using the rule described in §605.3, he earns three Quarters of Coverage. If the earnings and self-employment income were reversed, the outcome would be different. If he had $400.00 in wages but only $350.00 in net earnings from self-employment, he would receive only one Quarter of Coverage. The net earnings from self-employment are less than $400.00 and do not get added in at all; only his wages count. Because his wages are only one multiple of the minimum required for 1978 ($250.00) he receives only one Quarter of Coverage.

Chapter 7
Benefit Amounts

§ 705.5   Deductions to Recover an Overpayment
§ 705.6   Deductions for Medicare Premiums
§ 705.7   Rounding Down

§ 701 - Benefit Amounts in General

For obvious reasons, the way that the Social Security Administration computes the amount of benefits payable is very important to everyone. In this chapter we will discuss the rules which are used to figure benefits. We will discuss the basic computation, recomputation due to earnings after you first become entitled to benefits, reductions for age and for entitlement to other benefits, and the credits given for delayed retirement.

Deductions because of earnings are discussed in detail in Chapter 8. The method and timing of payments are discussed in Chapter 10.

§ 702 - Computations

§ 702.1 - The Primary Insurance Amount

The first step in figuring benefits is to determine the primary insurance amount (PIA). All benefits are based on it. The benefit amount for a retired worker at age 65 and for a disabled worker is equal to the primary insurance amount. It is reduced for retirement benefits before 65 and increased for delayed retirement.

Benefits for spouses, children and survivors are figured as a percentage of the primary insurance amount. The PIA is the single most important concept for computing benefit amounts.

§ 702.2 - The Basic Computation Formula

The primary insurance amount (PIA) is based on the earnings of the worker on whose account the benefits are claimed. The maximum PIA for a worker 65 in 1996 is $1,248. For a worker with average annual earnings of approximately $24,000, it is about $860, and for a low wage earner with average annual earnings of approximately $11,000, it is about $520.

There is one basic formula used to compute almost all PIA's. Some special formulas, used rarely, are discussed in §702.3. The basic formula is described in this section, but is extremely complicated and is almost always done by SSA's computers rather than manually.

The 1978 amendments to the Social Security Act mandated "indexing" of earnings to adjust earnings of earlier years for inflation occurring now. The first step of the basic computation formula is to index the worker's annual earnings for past years. Each year's earnings are separately indexed. To do this, SSA first determines the "indexing year." For retirement cases, this is the second year before the year the worker becomes age 62 (not necessarily the year of retirement). For disability cases it is the second year before the onset of disability and for survivor cases it is two years before the year of death. For example, for a worker who becomes age 62, disabled, or dies in 1995, the indexing year is 1993.

SSA then determines the "average annual earnings" of all workers for the indexing year and for each past year after 1950. They divide the "average earnings of all workers" for the indexing year by the "average earnings of all workers" for each prior year. They multiply the answer for each year by the amount of the worker's earnings for that prior year (but not more than the FICA maximum for that year). The result is the indexed earnings for each prior year. This process is for all years after 1950 up to, but not including, the indexing year. SSA uses actual earnings, not indexed earnings, for the indexing year and later years.

After the earnings for all years have been indexed (except the indexing and later years), SSA then determines how many years to use for the computation.

For people born before 1930, subtract 1951 from the year of attainment of age 62, onset of disability, or death - whichever is earliest. (People who become disabled at age 64 would still subtract 1951 from age 62 because that is earlier than the onset of disability). For people born in 1930 or later, add 22 to the year of birth. Subtract that figure from the year of attainment of age 62, onset of disability or death. For *retirement and survivor* benefits subtract 5. The result is the number of years used, called "computation years."

For *disability* benefits, if the onset of disability is age 26 or younger, do not subtract anything additional; ages 27 through 31, subtract 1; ages 32 through 36, subtract 2; ages 37 through 41, subtract 3; ages 42 through 46, subtract 4; age 47 or older subtract 5. The minimum number of computation years used is 2. The maximum number of computation years is 35.

Example: John becomes 65 in 1997. This means he attained age 62 in 1994. Subtract 1954 from 1994. The answer is 40. You then deduct 5. The result is 35. Use 35 computation years to figure John's primary insurance amount.

Bill was born in 1947 and died in 1993. Add 22 to 1947. The result is 1969. Subtract 1969 from 1993. The answer is 24. Deduct 5. Use 19 computation years.

Joe was born in 1951 and became disabled in 1994 at age 43. He became age 22 in 1973. Subtract 1973 from 1994. The answer is 21. Deduct 4. Use 17 computation years.

After determining the number of computation years, SSA looks at the annual indexed earnings calculated as described above from 1951 through the year before the year for which the benefit is calculated. You may include the year of death in survivor cases. Take the computation years with the highest indexed earnings, and add up the total indexed earnings for those computation years.

When recomputing a retirement benefit to include earnings after entitlement, the number of computation years is the same. If the earnings for the new year are higher than the indexed earnings of the lowest year used in the first computation, substitute the new year's earnings. When you add the new year's earnings into the total, you must subtract the lowest year's indexed earnings.

Once SSA has determined the total indexed earnings for the computation years, they divide by the number of months in the computation years. These are called "Divisor months." The number of computation years times 12 equals the divisor months used.

The total of the indexed earnings for the computation years used, divided by the divisor months, rounded to the next lower dollar, yields the "average indexed monthly earnings."

The primary insurance amount is a certain percentage of the average indexed monthly earnings. This varies depending on the average indexed monthly earnings and on the year for which the computation is being done. For example for 1992, the percentages are as follows: 90% of the first $387, plus 32% of the excess over $387 up to $2,333 of the average indexed monthly earnings, plus 15% of the average index monthly earnings over $2,333. The dollar amounts at which the percentages change are called "bend points." The percentages (90%, 32%, 15%) stay the same for each year, but the bend points change annually. They are determined by dividing the indexing year's average total wages of all workers, by the average total for 1977 ($9,779.44), and multiplying the result by $180.00 and $1,085.00 to give you the two bend points.

The bend points used depend on the first year of eligibility (i.e. the year the worker becomes 62, disabled or dies), and remain applicable for later recomputations, even though the recomputation is done in a later year.

Cost-of-Living Adjustments (§704.2) are added to the primary insurance amount beginning with the year of eligibility, effective with the month of increase.

Once the primary insurance amount is calculated, the benefit amount payable is determined according to the rules in this chapter, and by referring to the benefit amounts listed for each type of benefit in Chapter 2.

§ 702.3 - Other Computation Formulas

The basic computation formula discussed in the preceding section applies to almost all beneficiaries. Other computations are used in a very small number of cases which we will discuss briefly.

The 1977 amendments to the Social Security Act changed the basic computation formula to the "average indexed monthly earnings" method discussed in §702.2. The general effect of this change was to take inflation into account, but also to reduce the amount of benefits.

For workers who attained age 62 before 1984, Social Security may use a different formula. This other formula is called the "new-start transitional guarantee." When using this formula, however, Social Security does not add in earnings from the year you attained age 62 or later. This formula does not use indexed earnings; instead it uses the actual earnings. The transitional guarantee formula may result in a higher primary insurance amount in some cases where the last year's earnings were in 1980 or 1981.

If you had been entitled to Disability Insurance Benefits more than a year before your entitlement to Retirement Benefits, the year of your death in survivor cases or a second period of disability, you will receive the higher of a primary insurance amount figured under the basic computation formula or the primary insurance amount upon which your disability benefit was based. In other words, you will not have a lower primary insurance amount than you had while you were disabled.

The Social Security Administration also uses other formulas where there are little or no earnings after 1951. We will not discuss the details of these other formulas, but you should be aware that they may be used. As noted above, only a very small number of people will have a higher benefit under these other computation formulas. Social Security will automatically consider all computation formulas and give you the highest one.

§ 702.4 - The Effect of Having Years With No Earnings

As noted in §702.1 above, the years used in figuring the primary insurance amount are the years from 1951 or the year you turn 22, if later, through the year before the year you turn age 62. The lowest five years are dropped from that base period. If you have five or less years with no earnings shown on your earnings record, it will have no effect on your computation. However, if you have more than five years with no earnings, then it will, because the overall average monthly earnings during the computation will be less.

Generally, if the year with no earnings is a later year, it will have more of an effect than an earlier year. This is because the amount of earnings covered by Social Security have increased over the years, so that recent years' earnings subject to FICA (see Appendix 3) are very high, although "indexing" (see §702.1) has somewhat reduced the disparities.

§ 702.5 - How to Double-Check Your Benefit Amount

In the vast majority of cases, Social Security correctly computes your benefit amount, but sometimes mistakes occur. The most common mistake is the failure to include earnings for a given year. If earnings are not shown on your earnings record, it may affect the amount of your average monthly earnings and therefore the amount of your benefit.

If you doubt the accuracy of your benefit amount, the first thing to do is go to your Social Security office and ask them to obtain a copy of your earnings record used in the computation of the benefit. It may take them several weeks or a month to obtain this. You should check to make sure that the correct earnings are posted for each year. If there is a year which does not have earnings shown, determine if it makes a difference in the computation of your benefit. If it is one of the five lowest years in the computation period as discussed in §702.1 above, then it does not matter.

The general rule is that you can correct your earnings record only for the past three years. However, there are exceptions to this rule

(§1405). If you have a year with no earnings shown which is more than three years in the past, you can ask Social Security to re-check their records in Baltimore. This is called a "scout." If earnings turn up on the "scout" your benefit will be re-adjusted. If they do not turn up Social Security may still allow you to correct your earnings record if you have evidence of the earnings, such as W-2 form, pay stubs or a tax return.

If all your earnings are shown on your earnings record and you still doubt the accuracy of the benefit, you should ask a Claims Representative (§105) to show you how your benefit was computed step by step.

If you are not satisfied you have the right to request a reconsideration. This is part of the administration appeals process (see Chapter 13).

§ 703 - Reductions

§ 703.1 - Reductions for Age - Benefits Before Age 65

In General

In the case of retirement, aged wife's, aged widow's and disabled widow's benefits, your benefit amount will be reduced if you take the benefit before Normal Retirement Age, currently age 65. Beginning in 2003, Normal Retirement Age will gradually increase to age 66 by 2009, and then to age 67 by 2027.

The reduction is figured on a monthly basis, not yearly. There is a different reduction formula for retirement, wife's, and widow's benefits. These are discussed in a detail in the following sections.

Reduction for Age - Retirement Benefits

If you are entitled to a retirement benefit before the month you turn 65, the benefit must be reduced. The reduction factor goes by months, not by years, so that if your first month of entitlement is the month before you turn 65, the benefit is reduced by 1 month. If the first month of entitlement is 6 months before 65 it will be reduced 6 months and so forth all the way back to age 62 which is 36 reduction months, (but see §207.4).

The legal reduction factor is 5/9 of 1% of the primary insurance amount for each month you are entitled to a benefit before the month you turn 65. A full 36-month reduction comes out to 20%, but remember that the reduction factor goes by month, not by year. For example, if you were born in September 1919, you turn 65 in September 1984. If your entitlement to benefits starts in January 1983 your primary insurance amount is reduced by 20 reduction months because that is the number of months before the month you turn 65. If your primary insurance amount is $500.00, 1% of it is $5.00. 5/9 of 1% is $2.77. Multiply this amount by the number of reduction months. 20 times $2.77 is $55.40. The monthly benefit amount is $500.00 minus $55.40, which is $444.60. The actual amount payable to you is rounded down to the nearest dollar ($444.00). See §705.7.

A formula is used by Social Security to figure the monthly benefit amount instead of the above method. The formula is 180 minus the number of reduction months, times the primary insurance amount, divided by 180 or $[(180-RM) \times PIA)]/180$. Applying the facts in the example used above we take 180 and subtract 20, the number of reduction months. This leaves 160. Multiply 160 times the primary insurance amount of $500.00 which is 80,000. Divide by 180 and the answer is $444.44. This is rounded down to the nearest dollar for a final benefit amount of $444.00.

A third method of figuring the reduced benefit is to use the reduction factor listed in the chart at Appendix 8. The factor for 20 reduction months is .888. Using the above example, .888 multiply times 500 (the primary insurance amount) to arrive at a monthly benefit amount of $444.00.

You may note that there are some minor discrepancies in the results obtained by using the above formulas. The first formula is from the Social Security Act, the second is the one Social Security uses, and the third is published in Social Security pamphlets.

Please note that any reduction for age stays in effect until you turn 65. At that time the reduction factor is readjusted to exclude any reduction for months before 65 for which you do not receive a full monthly benefit (§704.4). If you receive all monthly benefits, the reduction stays in effect for life.

Reduction for Age - Spouse's Benefits

Benefits payable to a spouse of a retired or disabled worker are reduced if entitlement to the spouse's benefit begins before the month the spouse turns 65. Please note that if the wife is entitled because she has a child in her care (§207.8) there is no reduction for age. The spouse's benefit is reduced only for the spouse who is entitled because of her age.

If the spouse has worked under Social Security and is entitled to a retirement benefit on her own account see §302.

The reduction formula applicable to spouse's benefits is 25/36 of 1% of 1/2 of the worker's primary insurance amount for each month of entitlement to the spouse's benefit before 65. The reduction factor goes by months, not by years, so that the difference between taking a reduced benefit when you are 62 and 11 months and taking it when you are exactly 63 is 1 additional month of the reduction factor.

Example: Wanda is 63. She never worked under Social Security. Her husband is entitled to a benefit with a primary insurance amount of $600.00. Wanda becomes entitled to the spouse's benefits when she is 15 months under age 65. To figure her benefit amount we take 1/2 of her husband's primary insurance amount ($600.00 divided by 2 equals $300.00); 1% of $300.00 is $3.00; and 25/36 of $3.00 is $2.08. Multiply this amount times 15 reduction months for a figure of $31.20. This is subtracted from $300.00 to result in a monthly benefit amount of $268.80, rounded down to the nearest dollar of $268.00 (§705.7).

Now let's assume that Wanda worked under Social Security and has a primary insurance amount of $200.00. Her benefit would be figured as follows. First we take her own primary insurance amount and reduce it by 15 reduction months using the formula described in §708 above. The $200.00 is reduced because of her age to $183.30, rounded down to $183.00. We then determine her spouse's benefit and reduce it. The spouse's benefit is $100.00 (the difference between 1/2 of her husband's primary insurance amount and her own primary insurance amount). It is reduced 15 months using the formula described in this section. The $100.00 is reduced to $89.50, rounded down to $89.00. Her monthly benefit amount is composed of her own reduced benefit in the amount of $183.00 plus the reduced spouse's benefit in the amount of $89.00 for a total benefit payable of $272.00.

Instead of using the formula described above, another formula is used by Social Security. The formula is 144 minus the number of reduction months, times 1/2 of the worker's primary insurance amount, divided by 144, rounded down to the nearest dollar, or [(144-RM)x1/2 PIA]/144. Use the difference between 1/2 of the spouse's PIA and your own PIA if you are eligible on your own account.

Another method of figuring the spouse's benefit is to use a reduction factor from the chart in Appendix 8. Multiply 1/2 of the worker's primary insurance amount times the reduction factor corresponding to the number of reduction months. For example, the factor for 15 reduction months is .895. To figure Wanda's spouse's benefit from the above example (assuming she was not entitled to a benefit on her own account) take 300 (1/2 of her husband's primary insurance amount) times .895 to arrive at the reduced wife's benefit amount of $268.50, rounded down to $268.00.

Please note that the reduction stays in effect for all months before age 65, but then is readjusted to exclude a reduction for any month before age 65 for which no full monthly benefit is paid (§704.4). If all benefits before 65 are paid, the reduction stays in effect for life.

The maximum amount of the reduction for age based on 36 reduction months is 25%.

Reduction for Age - Widow's Benefits

Widows who are entitled to benefits because of age will have their benefit amounts reduced for any month before age 65 for which they are entitled to a benefit. For benefits payable before January, 1984, widows who were entitled to disabled widow's benefits before age 60 have an additional reduction at a rate different from the one which applies to widows who first become entitled at age 60. A disabled widow under 60 receives the same benefit amount as a widow at age 60, for benefits beginning January, 1984.

The formula specified in the Social Security Act for widow's benefits is a reduction of 19/40 of 1% of the primary insurance amount for each month before age 65 at the time entitlement begins. This works out to a 28 1/2% reduction at age 60. The reduction factor is based on the number of months before age 65, not the number of years. For instance, if you take a reduced widows benefit at age 62 1/2, the benefit will be reduced by 30 reduction months.

The formula used by Social Security to compute the widow's benefit amount is as follows: 4,000 minus (number of reduction months times 19), times the primary insurance amount, divided by 4,000, or [4,000-(19xRM)xPIA]/4000.

Regardless of the amount arrived at by using a reduction formula, the widow's benefit can never be greater than the amount of the monthly benefit which the husband received during his lifetime if he was entitled. For example, if the husband took a fully reduced benefit at exactly age 62, his primary insurance amount was reduced by 20%. The widow cannot receive more than that even if she first becomes entitled when she is 65. Likewise, any additional credit for delayed retirement (§704.6) is added to the benefit of the widow. For example, if the husband had a primary insurance amount of $500.00 which was increased by 3% due to delayed retirement, the widow's benefit would be figured using $515.00, the increased amount.

At age 65 the reduction factor is readjusted to exclude any reduction for a month before age 65 for which no full monthly benefit was actually paid (see §704.4). Note that a widow also receives a readjustment of the reduction factor at age 62 (see §704.5).

If a widow is entitled to a benefit based on her own account at age 62 she has an option to take either the reduced widow's benefit or the reduced retirement benefit on her own account and then switch over to the other benefit unreduced at age 65 or earlier (see §303).

For benefits payable before January 1984 to disabled widows under age 60 there is an additional reduction of 43/240 of 1% for each month of entitlement before age 60. This is in addition to the reduction which applies to entitlement for widows at age 60. For example, a disabled widow who first becomes entitled at exactly age 54 has the benefit reduced by 60 months at the regular reduction factor, plus 43/240 of 1% for the 72 months before age 60. Note that the additional reduction for a disabled widow has been eliminated for benefits payable beginning January 1984.

How Taking Reduced Retirement Benefit Will Affect Other Benefits

If you take a retirement benefit before age 65 and it is therefore reduced for age, it may have an effect on other benefits payable to you or to others. The most common example of this is the case of widow's benefits. If you take your own reduced retirement benefit and then die, the amount your widow may receive cannot exceed the amount you were receiving in your lifetime, although she is over age 65 at the time she first becomes entitled. She will however receive any cost of living adjustments which may occur after your death.

If at the time you apply for reduced retirement benefits you are also potentially eligible for spouse's benefits on a husband's or wife's account, you must apply for the reduced spouse's benefit as well, even if there are no benefits actually payable because of the husband's or wife's earnings. This provision only applies if at the time you make your application for reduced retirement benefits, your spouse is entitled to retirement or disability benefits. For example, your spouse turned 65 last year and is entitled to retirement benefits and Medicare.

However, due to his earnings no benefits are payable. You are 62 years old now and you apply for your own reduced retirement benefit. Social Security will require you to file an application for the reduced spouse's benefit if one half of the spouse's primary insurance amount is greater than your own primary insurance amount, regardless of whether cash benefits are payable to you as a spouse (your spouse's earnings will have no effect on the payment of your own benefits). If your spouse retires in 2 years, the additional spouse's benefit will be paid at the reduction rate in effect at the time you first applied for your own retirement benefits and not based on your age at the time the benefits are first payable, until you become 65 when the reduction will be adjusted (§704.4). See also §414.

If you are potentially eligible for widow's benefits at the time you file for reduced retirement benefits you do not necessarily have to apply for them. You have the option of taking one or the other benefit reduced and then switching over to the other one unreduced at age 65. See §303.

If you apply for reduced retirement benefits and you have a spouse who may be entitled on your account, the fact that your benefit is reduced for age has no bearing on determining the amount of the spouse's benefit. The spouse's benefit will be reduced according to her age at the time of the first entitlement. Your primary insurance amount will be reduced for the number of months you are under age 65 at the time of first entitlement; for the spouse, one half of your primary insurance amount will be reduced by the number of months she is under age 65 at the time she becomes entitled. See §§703.1.

If you become entitled to disability insurance benefits, the amount of your disability benefit will be reduced by the number of months you receive a retirement benefit before receiving a disability benefit. For example, let's say that you become disabled at age 63. No benefits are payable for the first 5 full months of the waiting period of your disability (§507). Because you are over age 62 you may receive reduced retirement benefits during the waiting period. The amount of that benefit is reduced for your age at the time you first become eligible for the retirement benefit. If you are exactly age 63 at that time, the primary insurance amount is reduced by 24 months using the reduction formula described in §703.1 above. When you become entitled to the disability benefit after your waiting period, the benefit amount will be readjusted to exclude reduction for any months for which you have not received a retirement benefit. Your disability benefit is reduced, but only by the number of retirement benefits you received before becoming eligible for the disability benefits.

Other benefits payable to dependents on your account will not be affected by the fact that you take reduced retirement benefits.

How Taking Reduced Widows Benefits Will Affect Your Own Benefit

If you take a widow's benefit before age 65 it may affect your own benefit depending on how old you were when you first took the widow's benefit. If you are 62 or older when first entitled to the widow's benefit it will have no effect on your own benefit and you may switch over at age 65 to your own benefit, unreduced, if that would yield a higher amount. This is discussed in full in §303.

However, if you take a reduced widow's benefit before age 62 it may have a permanent effect on your own retirement benefits. The amount of that reduction will be deducted from your own primary insurance amount at age 65. If you take your own benefit before 65, only one reduction will be imposed, either the regular retirement reduction (§703.1), or the dollar amount of the widow's reduction caused by receipt of widow's benefits for any month before age 62, whichever is higher. See also §704.5.

§ 703.2 - The Family Maximum

If there are dependents entitled to benefits on your account there is a maximum amount payable to your family unit regardless of what the full payment amounts to the dependents would be individually. This is referred to as the "family maximum." For example, in a case of a retired worker who has 3 children under age 18 entitled on his account, each child's benefit without taking the family maximum into account would be 50% of his primary insurance amount. However, depending on the amount of his primary insurance amount, there is a maximum which can be paid to the family regardless of the number of beneficiaries. Once this maximum is reached it does not matter how many additional dependents are entitled on the account because the total amount payable on the earnings record cannot exceed the family maximum. Each *dependent's* benefit is reduced proportionately so that the total for everyone does not exceed the family maximum. The worker's own benefit is never adjusted for this purpose.

The amount of the family maximum depends on the type of benefit you receive and the year in which you become 62, become disabled, or die, i.e., the "year of eligibility." The family maximums are the same for retirement cases and for survivor cases. There is a different family maximum applicable to disability cases.

In the case of retirement and survivor accounts, the family maximum goes on a sliding scale. The scale varies depending on the year of eligibility. "Bend points" are used in the same way that a primary insurance amount is derived from average indexed monthly earnings (see §702.2).

The family maximum is 150% of the primary insurance amount (PIA) up to the first bend point; plus 272% of the excess of the PIA over the first bend point up to the second bend point; plus 134% of the excess of the PIA over the second point up to the third bend point; plus 175% of the PIA in excess of the third bend point.

The percentages (150%, 272%, 134%, 175%) remain the same from year to year, but the bend points will change in the same way as the bend points used to compute the primary insurance amount (§702.2).

In disability cases, the family maximum is 85% of the average indexed monthly earnings (§702.2), but not more than 150% of the primary insurance amount, nor less than 100% of the primary insurance amount.

Once the amount of the family maximum is determined, the dependent's benefits are reduced proportionately so that the total family benefits do not exceed the maximum. In the case of retirement and disability benefits, the worker's primary insurance amount (not the benefit amount after age reduction) is deducted from the family maximum, and the balance divided among the dependents, in a proportion according to their original benefit amounts before any age reduction, as is the case with survivor benefits.

The adjustment for the family maximum is made after any deductions (See §705 of this chapter). If a dependent is not receiving benefits because of work deductions, the adjustment is made as if that dependent were not entitled on the account.

Where a person is entitled as a child on more than one account, the family maximums of both accounts are combined.

A divorced spouse's or a divorced widow's benefit is not reduced for the family maximum. Other dependent's benefits on the account are not reduced due to a divorced spouse's or widow's entitlement on that account.

§ 704 - Recomputations

§ 704.1 - Recomputations in General

At the time you first apply for Social Security benefits, a primary insurance amount is computed (§702.2) and a benefit amount determined.

This may be adjusted later under certain circumstances. Adjustments to the primary insurance amount or monthly benefit will affect benefits payable beginning with the effective date of the adjustment. There are four basic types of recomputations: cost of living increases, adjustments to include earnings after you first become entitled to a benefit, reduction factor adjustment at age 62 and age 65, and the delayed retirement credit which increases your benefit if you did not receive monthly benefits after age 65. These are discussed in detail in the following sections.

§ 704.2 - Cost of Living Increase

Each year all Social Security benefits are increased according to the cost of living increase which occurred during the preceding year. This is based on inflation as reflected in the Consumer Price Index. The cost of living increase is effective beginning with the month of December. Please note that monthly benefits are paid in arrears (§1003) so that the benefit increase effective with December is reflected in the monthly benefit check received in January of the following year.

The cost of living increases are shown in Appendix 5. The increase is computed as a percentage of the monthly benefit amount, not the primary insurance amount.

§ 704.3 - Adjustment for Earnings After Entitlement

As noted in §702.2 the primary insurance amount is based on your earnings ending with the year before the year you first become eligible, (survivor cases include the year of death). For example, if you apply for benefits in 1997, your earnings through 1996 will be included in the computation. However, if you work in the year you first become entitled to benefits or later and the earnings in the later year are greater than the lowest year's earnings in the computation of your benefit, then your primary insurance amount will be increased. If the amount of your earnings in the later year is less than the lowest year's earnings there will be no increase in your benefit. See §702.2.

The increase is effective with January of the year after the year of the additional earnings. If you continue working, and your annual earnings are greater than the lowest year used in the computation of your benefit, the increased benefit amount will be payable beginning with January of the following year.

This adjustment increases your primary insurance amount and accordingly will increase the benefit for anyone who is receiving benefits on your account.

Social Security will automatically readjust your benefit amount to include additional earnings if it yields a higher benefit. However, they are very backlogged in doing this. In fact, they run years behind. You may request an earlier readjustment.

§ 704.4 - Refiguring the Age Reduction at Age 65

If you received a benefit reduced for age (§703.1), the reduction factor will be adjusted effective with the month you become 65. This adjustment will eliminate the reduction for any month before 65 for which you did not receive a full monthly benefit. If you received all benefits, there is no adjustment. If you received a partial benefit for a month, the reduction attributable to that month's entitlement will be eliminated because you did not receive a *full* monthly benefit.

This reduction factor adjustment applies to all benefits which were reduced for age and is effective beginning with the month you turn 65. It cannot be figured until after the year you become 65 because the amount of your earnings may affect whether or not any benefits will be withheld for that year.

Example: John filed for reduced retirement benefits to be effective 15 months under 65. Accordingly, his primary insurance amount was reduced by 15 months. After he became entitled to reduced retirement benefits, he had earnings which prevented the payment of benefits for 6 full months and for part of a 7th month. When he turns 65, the primary insurance amount will be reduced permanently by only 8 months. The month he received partial payment is also eliminated. His benefit amount will increase accordingly. No adjustment will be made until after he files an annual report (§902.3) for the year he turns 65. When the recalculation is done, it will be retroactive to the month he turned 65.

§ 704.5 - Refiguring Age Reduction for Widows at Age 62

In addition to the reduction factor adjustment at 65 as described in §704.4, widows who received reduced widow's benefits before 62 are entitled to a readjustment of their benefit amount at 62 to eliminate a reduction factor for any month before 62 for which they did not receive a full monthly benefit. The increased monthly benefit will be payable beginning with the month you turn 62.

Example: Sally applies for widow's benefits at exactly age 60 and the widow's benefit is therefore reduced by 60 reduction months. She returns to work and has earnings which require 5 monthly benefits to be withheld and part of a 6th month before 62. The reduction factor based on 60 reduction months will be used to figure benefits payable up through the month before she becomes 62. However, beginning with the month she attains age 62, the reduction factor will be adjusted to eliminate the 6 months for which she did not receive a full monthly benefit before 62. If she works again between 62 and 65, the benefit amount will be adjusted again at 65 as described in §704.4.

§ 704.6 - Delayed Retirement Credits

If you continue to work after Normal Retirement Age (currently age 65) and your monthly benefits are withheld because of your earnings, you will receive a credit for each month beginning with the month you turn 65 for which you did not receive a full monthly benefit. The credit varies, depending on your year of birth, from 1/4 of 1% to 2/3 of 1% for each month beginning with the month of age 65 for which you do not receive your monthly benefit. This comes out to between 3% and 8% per year. The chart at Appendix 11 lists the percentages according to year of birth. The credit is payable beginning with January of the year following the year in which you did not receive the benefits. In addition to the delayed retirement credit, you may also be eligible for an adjustment because of your earnings after your first year of entitlement (see §704.3).

The delayed retirement credit will not affect the benefits of any dependents on your account, but if you die and leave a widow, the widow will be entitled to the delayed retirement credit.

You are eligible for the credit whether or not you file at 65. It will be computed when you start to receive benefits. No credit is granted for any period you are not fully insured (§602).

§ 704.7 - How to Expedite Adjustments for Earnings After Entitlement

As discussed in §704.3, the amount of your benefit may be increased if you have earnings after the first year you become eligible for benefits provided that those earnings are higher than the lowest year of earnings used in the computation of your benefit amount.

The increase due to earnings is payable beginning with January of the year following the year of the earnings.

Social Security will recompute this adjustment automatically. However, it will take them many months and probably years to do it. This is because there is a lag from the time you earn the wages until the time Social Security receives the report of your earnings and then acts on it to increase your benefit. You can expedite this process by making a special request. To do this, you will need your W-2 form (or tax return for the year if you were self-employed). You must go or write to your local District Office and show them your tax return or W-2. Ask that the earnings be refigured immediately instead of waiting for the automatic readjustment. Social Security will act upon your request and refigure your benefits although it may take several months. Whether you ask Social Security to do it immediately or you wait until they do it automatically, the adjustment will be retroactive to the first month after the year for which you had the earnings.

§ 705 - Deductions

§ 705.1 - Deductions in General

After your monthly benefit amount is calculated using the rules discussed in this chapter, Social Security may, under certain circumstances, withhold part or all of the monthly benefit. The major reasons for these deductions are discussed in the following sections. Please also note that the family maximum discussed in §703.2 may also cause a reduction of the amount of the benefit payable to a dependent or survivor. The deductions we discuss here apply to the actual benefit amount figured *after* taking into account any reductions for age or adding any credits for later earnings or delayed retirement.

§ 705.2 - Deductions Because of Earnings

If your earnings in a year during which you are entitled to monthly benefits are over the limits applicable to that year, then some or all monthly benefits must be withheld. The retirement test or the work test, as it is sometimes called, is discussed in full in Chapter 8. Once the amount of benefits to be withheld is determined by using the annual earnings test, full monthly benefits for that year will be withheld beginning with the first month during which you are entitled, unless you request prorating (see §803). For example, if based on your annual earnings and applying the work test, it is determined that $5,000.00 of monthly benefits must be withheld and your monthly benefit amount is $600.00, then your monthly benefit will be withheld until the $5,000.00 is reached. If you are eligible beginning with January to a monthly benefit of $600.00, then benefits for the months of January through September will be withheld in full. This would be $4,500.00 worth of benefits. An additional $500.00 must be withheld to satisfy the $5,000.00, therefore the benefit for the month of October will have the $500.00 deducted and only $100.00 will be payable to you.

If you first became entitled to benefits beginning with the month of June instead of the month of January, no monthly benefits would be payable to you at all for the year because 7 x $600.00 is only $4,200.00, which is less than the amount which must be withheld based on your annual earnings.

If you have dependents entitled on your account, the dependents' benefits will also be withheld if your earnings require (see §803). However, the earnings of a dependent will affect only that dependent's benefits and will not affect the benefits of anyone else who receives payments on the account.

§ 705.3 - Deductions from Disability Benefits for Worker's Compensation or Disability Payments

If you are entitled to a disability benefit and are also entitled to Worker's Compensation or certain other types of disability payments (see §§511-512), the combination of the Social Security benefit and Worker's Compensation benefit (or other disability payment which is subject to the offset provision) cannot exceed 80% of your average earnings. The way average earnings are figured for these purposes is discussed in §511.

The offset will also apply to any dependents who receive benefits on your account, offsetting their benefits before yours. For example, your average earnings were $1,000.00 per month; you are entitled to a $500.00 Social Security disability benefit; you have a child who is entitled to $250.00 on your account. You are also eligible for $350.00 per month in Worker's Compensation benefits. Eighty percent of your average earnings is $800.00, but the total of the Social Security benefits and the Worker's Compensation benefits is $1,100.00. Therefore, the $300.00 difference must be withheld. First the child's benefit will be withheld, then $50.00 of your own benefit, so that the total of the Social Security benefits and Worker's Compensation benefits does not exceed 80% of the average earnings.

§ 705.4 - Deductions from Spouse's and Widow's Benefits Due to a Government Pension

If you receive Social Security benefits as a wife or widow, the amount of your benefit is reduced if you receive a government pension based on your own earnings if the public employment in which you worked was not covered by Social Security.

This government pension offset does not apply if you were potentially eligible for entitlement to a Social Security benefit as a wife or as a widow as of January 1977 and you first became eligible to a government pension from December 1977 through November 1982, (whether or not you received it). If you were not potentially eligible to the Social Security benefit in January 1977, or you became eligible for your government pension in December of 1982 or later, 100% of your government pension is deducted from your wife's or widow's benefit.

Due to a change in the law in 1983, if you became eligible for your government pension in July, 1983 or later, (whether or not you actually receive it), the offset is only 2/3 of the government pension.

These offsets apply only to spouse's or widow's benefits and do not apply to benefits on your own earnings record. The government pension offset applies only if your public employment was not covered by Social Security.

§ 705.5 - Deductions to Recover an Overpayment

Overpayments are discussed in detail in Chapter 11. If it is determined that you have been overpaid, you may have to pay the overpayment back (see Chapter 11 for exceptions). If you are receiving Social Security benefits, benefits will be withheld to recover the overpayment.

This is discussed in §1114. Note that in the first instance, Social Security will advise you that they will withhold your full monthly benefit until the entire amount of the overpayment has been recovered.

However, you may request that less than the full monthly benefit be withheld. Generally, this request will be granted if the overpayment can be recovered within 3 years. For instance, you were overpaid $1,000.00 and are entitled to a monthly benefit in the amount of $500.00. Social Security will seek to recover the overpayment by withholding 2 months' benefits. However, you may request that only part of your monthly benefit be withheld to recover the overpayment and Social Security generally will allow you 36 months. Instead of having the $1,000.00 deducted from two full months' benefits, the sum of approximately $30.00 per month may be deducted from your monthly benefits to recover the $1,000.00. Social Security does not charge any interest on this installment method of paying back the overpayment (for a more complete discussion of overpayments, see Chapter 11).

§ 705.6 - Deductions for Medicare Premiums

The medical insurance part of Medicare (Part B) requires the payment of a monthly premium. The monthly premium may be higher if you did not apply for Medicare coverage timely (see §1203).

If you are covered by medical insurance under Medicare the premium will be deducted from your monthly benefits, if you are receiving them. Otherwise, you will be billed on a quarterly basis. When your benefits begin the premium will be deducted from the monthly benefit. If you have already paid a quarterly bill, you will receive a refund at a later date.

§ 705.7 - Rounding Down

After Social Security computes your benefit (and makes any required deduction) the resulting monthly benefit amount will be reduced to the lowest multiple of $1.00. Rounding down is done after all the other factors used in computing benefits have been applied, including the Medicare deduction.

The only time that rounding down is not the last step is in the case of combined benefits (§1004). In that case, each benefit amount is figured separately and rounded down separately. The rounded down amounts are then combined.

Chapter 8
Earnings Limitations

§ 801 - The Earnings Test in General

All beneficiaries, except those whose benefits are based on disability or are over 70, are subject to a loss of benefits if their earnings exceed certain limits. The way your earnings affect benefits is called the Work Test, the Retirement Test, or the Earnings Test. They are all the same. Although disabled workers are not affected by the work test, their spouses and children who receive benefits on their account are subject to it. The effect of a disabled beneficiary's earnings are discussed in §504.

If your yearly earnings are below certain annual limits, there is no effect on benefits. If they are over the annual limit, you lose one dollar in benefits for every two dollars over the limit if you are under 65 throughout the year, or one dollar for every three dollars over the limit if you are 65 or over during the year. The limits are different depending on your age (§§802.1-802.3), and year involved. There is also a monthly limit which applies usually for only one year (§804). The earnings limits for different years are listed in Appendix 6.

The earnings of a retired worker affect all dependents receiving benefits on his or her account. However, a dependent's earnings will not affect the worker or any other dependent on the same account. Likewise, the earnings of a person receiving survivor benefits will not affect anyone else on that account.

Only earned income is considered for these purposes (§805). Income such as dividends or interest is not included (§806). All earnings for the year are counted, even your earnings before you become eligible for benefits or after your entitlement ends. See §807 and §808 for special rules.

If you have a short taxable year, such as occurs when you switch from a calendar to a fiscal year, the annual earnings limit is prorated in the same way as the year of death (§810).

§ 802 - Earnings Limits

§ 802.1 - Earnings Limit - Under Age 65

If you will not reach age 65 during the year, you lose one dollar of benefits of every two dollars over the annual limit for that year, (Appendix 6). All earnings for the year are included, even those earned before your eligibility for benefits. Earnings limits are listed in Appendix 6. Note that you may receive benefits for any month your earnings are less than the monthly limit (§804), usually for only one year.

To determine the amount of benefits which must be withheld, subtract the yearly limit from your annual earnings and divide the remainder by two.

§ 802.2 - Earnings Limit - Ages 65 to 69

If you become age 65 at any time during the year, you lose one dollar in benefits for every three dollars over the annual limit (Appendix 6).

All earnings for the year are included, even those earned before or after your eligibility for benefits. Note that you may receive benefits for any month your earnings are less than the monthly limit (§804), usually for only one year.

To determine the amount of benefits which must be withheld, subtract the yearly limit from your annual earnings, and divide the remainder by three.

§ 802.3 - Earnings Limit - Age 70 and Over

Beginning the month you attain age 70, you can earn as much as you like and still collect all your Social Security benefits. As soon as you turn 70, there is no earnings limit. For the year you turn 70, if you are an employee, only the amount of money you earn through the month before the month you turn 70 will count. For example, if you turn 70 in July, only your earnings from January 1st through June 30th are included for the work test. You should not report your earnings from July 1 on. If you are self-employed, divide your annual earnings by 12 and then multiply the answer by the number of months before the month you reached 70.

For example, Paul attained age 70 on August 5, 1996; he was self-employed all year and had net earnings from self-employment of $18,000.00. Divide the $18,000.00 by 12 to arrive at the amount of $1,500.00. Multiply the $1,500.00 by 7 (the number of months in the year before you turned age 70). He should report $10,500.00 in self-employment earnings, because only this amount will affect benefits.

§ 803 - How Earnings Are Charged Against Monthly Benefits

Whenever you earn over the yearly exempt amount, Social Security will withhold the required amount (§801) of Social Security benefits beginning with the earliest month of entitlement. Social Security will withhold full monthly benefits until the entire amount that has to be withheld for the year is withheld (see §806 for exceptions). They do not prorate the withholding over the course of the year, (unless you request this - see below) they withhold all benefits beginning with the first month of eligibility, until the full required amount has been withheld.

For example, Harold, age 68, is entitled to $500.00 a month from Social Security. He expects to have excess earnings requiring $1,200.00 to be withheld from his Social Security benefits. Social Security will withhold his entire checks for January and February. They will withhold $200.00 for March, and pay him $300.00 for that month. He will receive his full $500.00 benefit for the months of April through December. All the withholding is done before any benefits are paid to him.

If one or more dependents receives benefits on your account, any partial payment is allocated to each beneficiary proportionate to his share of the total family benefits.

Using the above example, assume Harold had a wife Beatrice, who is over 65, not working and entitled to $250.00 a month on Harold's account. The $1,200.00 to be withheld would be withheld as follows: January - Harold, $500.00; Beatrice $250.00; February - Beatrice, $150.00; Harold, $300.00. Harold would receive a check for $200.00 for February and Beatrice would receive a check for $100.00. Both would receive full checks for March through December.

If Beatrice had excess earnings instead of Harold, only her benefits would be withheld. A dependent's earnings will never require withholding of the worker's or another dependent's benefits. Likewise, the excess earnings of a survivor will not affect another survivor's benefits.

Excess earnings are not carried over to another year. Only the benefits payable in the year of the earnings are subject to withholding. See §806 regarding the monthly earnings test.

§ 803.1 - Pro-Rating

Although Social Security procedures usually require full withholding of benefits until all required benefits are withheld, you may request that the withholding of benefits be prorated over the course of the year. Instead of receiving *no* benefits for the normal withholding period and the full benefits, you may choose to receive *partial* benefits.

In the example above, the $1,200.00 to be withheld could be spread over 12 months at $100.00 deducted from each month's benefits instead of waiting until March to receive any benefits.

If the period for prorating does not extend into the following year, your written request for prorating will be granted. Prorating of work suspensions will not be granted if you have an existing overpayment (§1101).

Prorating may be extended up to June of the following year, but only if you claim that loss of benefits will cause a financial hardship, or require you to significantly revise your retirement plans. Social Security will ask you to explain this in writing. Additionally, there must be no expectation that you will have earnings over the limit in the following year.

In limited situations, you may request that current year work suspensions be deferred completely to the next year.

This request will be granted only if you claim *extreme* financial hardship unless you receive full payments for a limited time until your financial situation improves at a time when you can better do without your benefits. The recovery of the deferred deductions must be accomplished by June of the following year. This request will not be granted if you have an existing overpayment or if you expect to earn over the limit in the following year.

§ 804 - The Monthly Earnings Test

If your earnings for a year are over the applicable earnings limits, (Appendix 6) Social Security will determine the amount of benefits which must be withheld. No benefits will be withheld from a "non-service" month, no matter how high the annual earnings may be. The way non-service months are determined is called the Monthly Earnings Test. Under this rule, you have a non-service month for any month after entitlement in which you earn under a certain amount, if you are an employee. If you are self-employed, the test is whether you render substantial services to your business. The monthly limits for employees vary depending on your age and the year involved.

Amounts are listed in Appendix 6.

If you are self-employed, the dollar limits do not apply. Instead, the "substantial services" rule is used. Generally, if you spend more than 45 hours per month at your business, your services are considered substantial. If you work less hours per month, the services are not substantial and you may have a non-service month. If your business is highly remunerative, such as a lawyer, doctor, consultant, etc. more than 15 hours per month is considered substantial.

You may be eligible for more than one non-service month in a year, but you are not eligible for non-service months in more than one year (with some exceptions to be discussed). The year in which you are eligible for non-service months is called a "grace year." It is the first year in which you have a non-service month. This is not necessarily the first year you are entitled to benefits.

Example: John turns 65 in 1995 and applies for benefits. Although he continues working and earns over the monthly amount in all months of 1995, some benefits are payable because the amount to be withheld based on his yearly earnings is less than the total of his benefits for the year (See §408 for a discussion of how this works). Because he has no non-service months in 1995 this is not a grace year. He has even higher earnings in 1996, enough to require withholding of all benefits. However, he earns under the monthly limit during the months of August and September. Because these are non-service months, he is paid his benefits for those months despite his annual earnings. 1996 is his grace year. He works in 1997 and again his earnings require withholding of all benefits. He has no earnings in July, August or September, but these benefits are withheld based on his annual earnings because he has already used his grace year.

There are two situations where certain beneficiaries are entitled to a second grace year. The first case applies to a child, a Young Wife (§204.2) or a Young Widow (§204.7). These beneficiaries receive a second grace year for the year in which their entitlement terminates, unless the termination is due to death or change to another type of benefit with no break in entitlement.

The second case applies to any beneficiary who receives one type of benefit which terminates, but then becomes entitled to another type of benefit with at least a one month break entitlement. The first year with a non-service month during which the beneficiary is entitled to the second benefit is a grace year.

§ 805 - Income That Counts

Under the annual earnings test, your earnings are the sum of gross wages plus net earnings from self-employment, minus any net loss from self-employment.

Wages are counted even if they are not covered by Social Security tax (FICA). Bonuses and awards are counted if they were actually earned during the year. Advances against future commissions are counted if you are an employee.

Dividends and interest received by a dealer in stocks and securities are counted if produced by his inventory for resale. Profit-sharing payments from a plan which is not tax-exempt are included. Real estate dealers who hold property for resale must include rental income from such property.

Royalties received from a copyright or patent obtained in or after the year you turn 65 are counted for deduction purposes. However, royalties received from such property obtained before the year you turn 65 are not counted beginning with the year you turn 65.

Sick pay received during the first six months after stopping work is included, as well as temporary disability insurance, unless you paid the premiums for it.

Travel and business expenses paid to an employee are counted, unless they are specifically identified as such at the time the payment is made. Vacation pay is counted, but if it is paid at or after the termination of employment and is attributable to a prior year, it may not be counted for the current year's earnings.

Before 1984, payments of idle-time, standby, "subject to call" and other such payments for a non-work period after age 62 were not counted for the work test. Beginning January 1, 1984, these types of payments are included as earnings.

§ 806 - Income That Doesn't Count

Payments which do not represent wages or self-employment income are not included for purposes of the retirement test. You do not count such items as interest, dividends, capital gains, legal damages (unless they result from a legal action for wages), wages which are used to hire a substitute employee, rental income, income from a hobby, prizes and awards, royalties from a work personally created on which a patent or copyright was obtained before the year you turn 65 if the royalties are received in or after the year you turn 65, sick pay received more than six months from the last month you worked, unemployment benefits and worker's compensation benefits.

Certain self-employment income may be excluded, see §808.

Although a particular payment may be considered wages for deduction purposes, if it is attributable to a time before your entitlement it may not affect your benefits. See the next section.

§ 807 - When Earnings are Counted

Wages are counted as earnings for the year in which they were earned. It is presumed that wages paid in a year were earned in that year, unless you show otherwise. Self-employment income is earned when received (or accrued, for those on the accrual method), regardless of when the services were rendered.

Sometimes special payments are made at or near retirement, such as advances, back pay, bonuses, severance pay, accrued vacation pay, holiday pay and so forth. If these payments were earned in an earlier year, they are not included in the earnings test for the year of retirement. Likewise, the month in which such a payment is earned may be important for determining non-service months (§804).

If your employment has not ended, payments for sick pay, holiday pay, and vacation pay are earned at the time of your *absence*. Advances against commissions, payment in lieu of vacation and occasional bonuses are considered earned in the *month of payment*. If you can establish that they should be attributed to a different period, Social Security will do so. Back pay, regular bonuses and school teacher's summer pay is considered earned in the month for which payment is made.

If the payment is made at the time of or after your employment terminates, the wages are considered earned as of the last month worked. However, if it is clear from a written plan that the payment relates to an earlier period, it will not be counted as earnings for the current period. For example, if you have accrued a month's vacation which you could have taken in an earlier year, you do not include that as earnings for the retirement test when you are paid for that vacation time upon your retirement.

See the next section for a discussion of the self-employment income exclusion.

§ 808 - Self-Employment Income and Losses

Net losses from self-employment may be deducted from gross wages and other self-employment income for the year.

Example: Jim is a plumber. He earns $10,000.00 in wages. He also is self-employed in a plumbing business. He has $7,000.00 in net losses in his business. Only $3,000.00 is counted as earnings for the retirement test.

For purposes of the retirement test, you may exclude all self-employment income attributable to services rendered before your first month of entitlement, but received (or accrued for those who use that method) in a year after the first year of entitlement. For example, if your first month of entitlement is December, 1994, you may exclude from 1995's earnings (for the retirement test only) that income which is attributable to services performed before December, 1994.

§ 809 - Special Problems for Business Owners

As a business owner, it is easy for you to reduce your salary when you reach retirement age to qualify for benefits even if you do not actually retire. Social Security has special procedures for retirement claims from people who own a business. They will not simply accept your word that your earnings are below the earnings limit.

Social Security will assume that your earnings are over the limit unless you can prove to their satisfaction that your actual services have been reduced.

If you have sold your business they will want to see the contract and other documents to make sure it is a bonafide transaction and not merely a sham solely designed to make you eligible for benefits without really retiring.

If you will continue in the business, they will want an explanation of why your income is reduced. Any reduction in income must correspond to a reduction in your services. Stopping or cutting your salary, without a reduction in your duties, is not sufficient. They will want to know who will assume your former duties, and what qualifications they have to do it.

Social Security will require you to give a signed statement detailing the nature of your business, your pre-retirement and post-retirement duties, the names and addresses of your major customers and suppliers, how many hours you will spend at the business and on what days, what kinds of payments you receive from the business and how much.

They will require you to submit your personal and business tax returns for the last two or three years, and any other records they believe important, depending on your type of business.

They will check up on the statements you give. They will call your suppliers and customers to see if you are still personally dealing with them. A Field Representative (§105) may call at your place of business posing as a customer to see if you are there and if you are working. They will scrutinize your tax returns to see if you are overstating deductions or taking money out of the business in a disguised form.

Social Security does all this to prevent payment of retirement benefits to someone who has not really retired. If they decide that your retirement is questionable, they will not pay you.

Before you file for benefits, if you are not selling or closing your business, you must be prepared to explain, in full detail, why your earnings will be less, and who is taking over your duties. Expect them to confirm everything you tell them. Even if they start your checks, they may reevaluate your case in three months, six months or a year. If they do and then decide you were never really retired, they may claim that they overpaid you and require a refund.

A consultation with a lawyer with Social Security experience would be wise. You should do this *before* you go to the Social Security office. You are within your rights to intentionally restrict your earnings to qualify for benefits if you wish, but your earnings must be fairly related to your actual services.

§ 810 - Special Rule For the Year of Death

When a beneficiary dies, the annual earnings limit for the year is prorated according to the number of months during which the beneficiary was alive. If the beneficiary dies in the year of his 65th birthday before the month of that birthday, the under 65 annual limit (§802.1) is prorated. If he dies in the month of the 65th birthday (whether before or after the birthday) or later, the over 65 limit is used (§802.3).

Example: William's 65th birthday is September 27. He dies September 5. His annual earnings limit is 9/12 of the applicable yearly limit (Appendix 6).

§ 811 - Work Outside the U.S.

If you work in a foreign country for seven or more days in any one month your benefit is suspended for that month, unless the work is covered by U.S. social security tax. It doesn't matter how much your earnings are, even if the totals for the year or month are under the regular limits (§§801-802.3). Benefits for any dependent on your account are also suspended.

Chapter 9
Reporting Requirements

§ 901 - Reporting Requirements in General

After you have become entitled to Social Security benefits, you must report to the Social Security Administration any change that may affect your continued eligibility to receive benefits. For all types of beneficiaries, earnings must be reported if they go over the earnings limits for the year, except those who receive benefits on account of disability (see Chapter 8 for a full discussion of the annual earnings limitations). In addition to earnings, anything else which affects benefits must be reported, including marriage, remarriage or divorce, not having a young child in your care for a month, stopping school attendance, or in some cases residing in certain foreign countries. Most common times will be discussed in the following sections.

§ 902 - Reporting Earnings

§ 902.1 - Reporting Earnings in General

Chapter 8 has a full discussion of the annual earnings limitations. The amount of money you are allowed to earn without any effect on your benefits depends on how old you are'and which year is involved. There are special reporting requirements for disability cases. This is discussed in §908 below.

If you receive benefits for another, for example, a mother who receives benefits for a child, it is your responsibility to report the earnings for that person.

Earnings can be reported to the Social Security Administration by a telephone call to the local district office or by a letter. If you have earned over the allowed amount for a year during which you have received benefits, you will be required to file an annual report of earnings (see §902.3).

§ 902.2 - When to Report Earnings

When you file a claim for Social Security benefits, you will be asked how much you expect to earn during that year. Additionally, if you file in the last three months of a year, you will be asked to estimate how much you expect to earn in the following year. The benefits paid to you will be based upon your estimates. Likewise, when you file an annual report of earnings (§902.3) you will be asked how much you expect to· earn in the coming year and your benefits will be based on that. If you estimate that you will earn under the exempt amount for a year you will be paid all benefits due. If you say you will earn over the exempt amount, Social Security will deduct the required amount from your monthly payments. (See §803.)

If you later expect that your earnings will be different than what you reported to Social Security, you should notify them immediately. If your earnings will be higher, you may be overpaid and have to pay money back (overpayments are discussed in full in Chapter 11). If you will earn less, you may be delayed in receiving money due you if you do not notify them promptly.

Sometimes people report that they will not earn over the limit for the year, but then it turns out that they do. Many people think that they don't have to tell Social Security until they actually earn over the limit.

This is incorrect and could result in an overpayment. You should notify Social Security at the time you *expect* your earnings to go over the limit, not when they actually do. Except for annual reports of earnings (§903), there are no formal requirements for notifying Social Security of an expected change in your earnings. You may call them on the phone, write a letter, or visit the District Office. If you write, address your letter to the attention of the "Service Unit" and include your claim number (§1407). The letter should be mailed to your local District Office (§105).

There are no penalties for not notifying Social Security about a change in your earnings estimate, but you must file an annual report for the year if your earnings are over the limit. You may be overpaid and have to pay money back if you delay telling Social Security about an increase in your earnings.

§ 902.3 - Annual Report of Earnings

If you receive any Social Security benefits during a calendar year and your earnings for that year were over the exempt amount, you are required by law to file an annual report of earnings and you may be penalized if you do not. If you did not earn over the limit, you do not have to file an annual report. The earnings limitations are discussed in full in Chapter 8. If you are entitled to benefits, but were not paid them, you should file an annual report even if your earnings are less than what you told Social Security. If you do not file an annual report in that case, you may not get those benefits for many years.

It is possible to have substantial earnings for a year and still be entitled to some Social Security benefits, especially if a wife is also entitled on the account.

The annual report must be filed no later than April 15 of the year following the year involved. If you are on a fiscal year basis, the annual report must be filed no later than three months and fifteen days after the end of your fiscal year.

Social Security regularly mails annual report forms to beneficiaries who received benefits during the year. However, you are responsible for filing the annual report even if you are not sent the form. The annual report may be filed with any district office, or mailed to the address on the form.

There are two annual report forms. One form asks only two questions: How much did you earn in the year being reported, and how much do you expect to earn in the current year. Benefits will be paid to you for the current year based on the estimate you put in the form. The other form asks an additional question about the amount of your monthly earnings for the year being reported. As noted in §804, every beneficiary is entitled to one year during which the benefits may be paid for a month with earnings less than the monthly exempt amount no matter how high the annual earnings are. You may only use this monthly earnings test during one calendar year. This is referred to as the "grace year." If you have not used a grace year you will be sent the annual report form which asks about the monthly earnings.

Penalties may be imposed if you do not file the annual report on time (§903).

§ 903 - Late Filing - Penalties

If you do not file your annual report of earnings by the deadline (usually April 15 of the following year, see §903) you will be subject to penalties if you were overpaid during the year in question.

The amount of the penalty is equal to one month's benefit if this is the first time you failed to file the annual report on time. If this is the second time, the penalty will be equal to two month's benefits. If it is the third time or more, the penalty will be three months' benefits. Social Security uses the benefit amount for December of the year involved for the penalty. If the amount of money overpaid for the year is less than the monthly benefit amount for the December benefit, the penalty will be equal to the amount you were overpaid. For example, if you were overpaid only $100.00, the penalty will be $100.00, instead of the monthly benefit amount (minimum of $10.00) but only for the first time you fail to file an annual report. For a second or later failure, the normal penalty may be less if the amount of your overpayment could have been deducted from a lesser number of months' benefits. In that case the penalty will be equal to only the number of months which would have had deductions because of the earnings. For example, a beneficiary with a monthly benefit rate of $400.00 per month has an overpayment of $600.00. This is the *third* time he has failed to file his annual report. The penalty for failure to file will be equal to only *two* months of benefits ($800.00) because the $600.00 overpayment would have caused deductions in only two months.

If you were paid the correct amount of benefits for the year being reported, or if money is due for the year being reported, there is no penalty for filing a late report of annual earnings.

If you can establish that you had good cause for not filing timely, there will be no penalty. Generally good cause can be found only if you took all reasonable steps to comply with your responsibility, or you were prevented from filing due to circumstances beyond your control, such as a physical or mental condition.

§ 904 - Reporting Changes in Marital Status

If you receive spouse's, widow's or child's benefits you must report any change in your marital status. If you become divorced from the worker, although you may be eligible to continue receiving benefits as a divorced wife, you must report the divorce anyway. If you were married to the worker for ten years and are at least 62, you may still receive benefits (see §204.3).

If you receive benefits as a divorced wife or widow, you must report a remarriage. Divorced widows who re-marry after age 60 (or after age 50 is disabled) may continue to receive benefits, the same as non-divorced widows who remarry after age 60. Widow's benefits will not be terminated due to remarriage if it occurs after age 60. You should nevertheless report it for the record, to change your name and identification code (§1407).

If a person who receives a child's benefit marries, the benefits will usually terminate. This must be reported to Social Security.

If one Social Security beneficiary marries another, (depending on which types of beneficiaries) the benefits may not terminate even though they would if the marriage did not occur between beneficiaries. A chart is located at Appendix 10 which tells you whether or not benefits will terminate due to remarriage.

If you receive child's benefits as a stepchild, you do not have to report the divorce of your natural parent and your stepparent. This will not affect the stepchild's eligibility. Once the stepchild is entitled to benefits on the stepparent's account, the benefits will continue despite a divorce.

If you receive benefits only on your own account, you do not have to report any change in your marital status, unless you wish a name change.

§ 905 - Reporting Changes in Student Status

As noted in §205.1 and in §409.1, a child may continue to receive child's benefits after age 18 if he is a full time student in certain cases. If you are receiving benefits on this basis, you must report any change in your full time school status. If you are over age 18 and no longer a full time student your benefits will terminate.

§ 906 - Reporting Child Not in Care

If you receive spouse's or widow's benefits because you have a child in your care, (see §207.8) your monthly benefit will be suspended for any month you do not have the child in your care. This does not terminate your benefits, it only suspends them (see §1008). You must report this to Social Security. Short absences of less than one month do not count. Only if the child is gone for the entire month must it be reported to Social Security. If the child goes away on vacation your benefits will not be suspended if you are still responsible for the child's upbringing and exercising parenting control and supervision. However, if the child goes to live with *another parent* for more than one month, you must report because it will result in suspension of your benefits for that month.

A penalty may be imposed for failing to report not having a child in your care. The penalty amount is equal to the benefit amount for the first month of a period in which the child is not in your care. The penalty for a second failure is twice the benefit amount. The penalty for a third subsequent failure is three times the benefit amount. The penalty cannot exceed the amount of benefits which should have been suspended.

§ 907 - Reporting Death

The death of a Social Security beneficiary should be reported immediately. A check received after the death of a beneficiary cannot be cashed. It must be returned to the Social Security Administration. If you cash a check for a beneficiary who has died, you may be subject to criminal penalties. A benefit is not payable for the month of death. A check received after the death may be due for an earlier month; if so, it must be reissued by Social Security. It cannot be cashed (see §1408).

In the case of a husband and wife who receive a combined check, it should be brought to the local Social Security District Office. A service representative or a claim representative will stamp the back of the check with a special endorsement called a "superendorsement" which will make it payable to the surviving beneficiary. You can then cash the check. Social Security will adjust your future benefits to take this into account.

§ 908 - Reporting Changes in Disability Cases

People who receive benefits because they are disabled do not have to file an annual report of earnings because the annual earnings limitations do not apply in disability cases. The earnings test *does* apply to spouses or children of disabled workers. Any work activity by a disabled beneficiary should be reported immediately to Social Security, regardless of the amount of earnings expected to be earned. The fact that you are working may have an effect on your continued eligibility to receive disability benefits (see §504).

If you receive benefits because of disability, you should report any medical improvement in your condition because you may no longer be totally disabled. There is no penalty for failure to report a medical improvement.

§ 909 - Reporting Work Outside the U.S.

You must report to Social Security as soon as you have worked seven or more days in one month in a foreign country (see §811). You are subject to a penalty for failing to report in the same way as penalties are imposed for failing to report that a child is not in your care (see Supplement §906).

Chapter 10
Payment, Non-Payment and Non-Receipt of Checks

§ 1001 - Checks in General

Social Security benefits are issued by the Treasury Department on regular green government checks. The check will have the Social Security number of the worker on whose account the benefits are based and will also have the beneficiary identification code which indicates which type of benefit you are receiving (§1407). The checks can be mailed to your home, to your post office box, or directly to your bank (§1006). Social Security benefits are not assignable and are not subject to attachment or levy by creditors. You can have them sent in care of someone else for mailing purposes, but Social Security will want an explanation. They want to make sure that no one else is depriving you of your Social Security benefits.

§ 1002 - The First Check

When you apply for Social Security benefits you may be required to submit certain documents (Chapter 4). After you have submitted everything required, you should receive your first check in about one month. This is the average processing time. Sometimes it takes as little as ten or 15 days; sometimes it can take up to three months. It is rare, but occasionally a case can take more than three months before the first check is sent out. Of course, the check will not be paid until it is due. If you apply in advance of the time you are first eligible for benefits, you will not receive it until you have met the eligibility requirement. For instance, if you apply for retirement benefits three months before you turn 62, you will not receive the check until that time. Remember that checks are paid in arrears (§1003).

If you have applied for Social Security benefits after the first month in which you are entitled, the first check may include retroactive benefits due for the past period. There is a full discussion of applications and retroactivity in Chapter 4.

Social Security has different procedures and systems for processing cases. Some cases can go through a computer system, other cases cannot. The cases which can go through the computer are processed much more quickly than the others. About a month after you apply for benefits, you can call the local district office to find out when you may expect to receive the first check. They usually will not be able to tell you how long it will take until approximately four weeks after you apply. They will be able to tell you at that time whether you can expect it within a few weeks, or if it could take a few more months.

§ 1003 - Regular Monthly Checks

After you have become entitled to Social Security benefits you will receive your checks on a monthly basis. The checks are paid one month in arrears. This means for example, that the check you receive in May is the benefit due for the month of April. The checks are paid on the third day of the month unless the third is a Saturday, Sunday or a holiday, in which case it will be paid before the third.

Always remember that the check you receive on the third of the month is the benefit due for the *preceding* month: *benefits are paid in arrears.*

§ 1004 - Combined Checks

If two or more people who live in the same household receive benefits on the same account, the Social Security Administration will usually combine the payments for each beneficiary into one monthly check (but not a parent and child). For example, if a husband and wife are both receiving benefits on the husband's account, they will get one monthly check, which will have both their names on it.

If the wife had worked on her own record and is entitled to benefits on her own account in addition to the wife's benefits, the checks will not be combined; each person will receive his and her own check. If you do not want your benefits combined into one check, you may request that they be issued separately.

If you receive combined payments in one check and one beneficiary should die, the surviving beneficiary can take the check to the local Social Security district office to have it made payable to him or her. The amount of benefits will be adjusted at a later time, although this may take several months.

§ 1005 - Special Checks

After you are receiving your regular monthly checks, you may be due an increase for different reasons (§704). If Social Security increases your benefit amount after the time you are first entitled to the increase, you will receive the increases for each unpaid month retroactively in one check. For example, let's say that you worked after you first became eligible for Social Security benefits. Your earnings may increase your benefit amount (§704.3).

Social Security will automatically recompute your benefit, but it may take them years to do it. If you first became eligible for Social Security benefits in 1993, but you worked in 1994, your earnings may cause your benefit amount to be increased for 1995 and later. Social Security may not recompute your benefit amount until 1996. You are due the increase beginning with 1995, the year after the earnings, so when Social Security gets around to it, you will be due money for 1995 and for the months in 1996 before the recomputation. They will send you a check which includes the increases for all those months. This check will be in an odd amount and can arrive at any time during the month, or the money can be combined with a regular check. You will usually receive a letter explaining why you are receiving the check or the odd payment, but the letter may come after you receive the check. It should come within about two weeks either before or after. If you receive an odd check and you do not yet have an explanation letter within two weeks, contact your Social Security office.

§ 1006 - Direct Deposit

If you wish, you can have your Social Security checks sent directly to your bank instead of to your home. This can be very convenient for obvious reasons. You must be receiving regular monthly checks. To arrange for this you must contact your bank, not the District Office. The bank must fill out certain forms and they will notify Social Security. It may take up to 3 months. If it doesn't start within that time, get a copy of the form from the bank and bring it to the District Office. They can make the computer inputs from the copy.

§ 1007 - Non-Payment in General

Regular monthly checks will stop if Social Security determines that your eligibility has terminated (§1009) or that you are subject to suspension (§1008). Before the benefits actually stop you should receive notice of Social Security's intention to terminate or suspend your benefits. You generally have a right to appeal these decisions. (See Chapter 13).

Sometimes you may receive only a partial benefit for the month. If you must pay back money because you have been overpaid, you may arrange for deductions from your monthly benefits over a period of time instead of withholding the full benefit amount until the overpayment is recovered.

If you are due a check for a month but you do not receive it, you should follow the guidelines in §1011.

§ 1008 - Suspension of Benefits

In some cases, even though you remain legally entitled to benefits, the payment may be suspended. The most common example of this is where benefits are suspended because of earnings. There is a full discussion of the Work Test in Chapter 8.

If you are a young wife or a young widow (eligibility based on having a child in your care) you are subject to a suspension of benefits for any full month you do not have a child who is entitled to benefits on the same account "in your care." Temporary absences do not count. If you child is away on vacation with relatives or at a boarding school, you are considered to have a child in your care if you are exercising parental control and responsibility over the child. If you are separated from the other parent, you are subject to suspension for any month the child is with that parent. Social Security looks at the calendar months involved and not the total number of days. If the child is in your care for at least one day during a calendar month, the benefit will not be suspended.

Another common reason for suspension of benefits is in the case of a spouse or a widow(er) who is eligible for a governmental pension based on his or her own earnings (§705.4). Before July, 1983 there is a dollar for dollar offset. If the governmental pension is greater than the Social Security benefit, no Social Security benefits is payable. Beginning with July 1983, only two-thirds of the governmental pension offsets Social Security benefits.

If your benefits are in suspense you are still legally entitled although you will not receive the benefit for any suspense month. Once the event causing suspense stops, your benefits can be resumed without the need for another application. You will notify Social Security of the change and the benefits will be started again.

§ 1009 - Termination of Benefits

In Chapter 2, each type of Social Security benefit is specifically described including the events which will terminate benefits. Benefits terminate upon death, and sometimes will terminate upon divorce, or marriage. Disability benefits may terminate if there is a medical recovery or you return to work.

Whatever the cause, benefits terminate the month before the month of the occurrence of the terminating event. For instance, in the case of death, if a beneficiary dies in the month of August the benefits terminate with the month of July. This sounds strange, but it really isn't. Remember that checks are paid in arrears so that the payment received in August is actually the payment for July. In all cases except disability (§513), the benefit is payable for the month of termination so that although the benefits terminate the month before the month of the event, the check is payable for the terminating month. In the case of the beneficiary who dies in August, the August 3rd check which is payable for the month of July is due and payable. The September 3rd check which would otherwise be due for the month of August is not payable and must be returned.

These rules apply to all types of events causing termination of benefits including death, marriage, remarriage, etc. Disability benefits may stop because you have returned to work or because you have made a medical recovery. In these cases, the termination of benefits occurs two months after the month the disability ceases. For example, if your disability ceases because of a medical improvement in June the termination applies to the month of August. Benefits are payable for the month of June, July and August, but not after August because that is the month of termination.

If you appeal a decision to terminate your disability benefits, you may request your benefits to continue until you receive a hearing (§1305). If you have had a hearing but your case is still under appeal, it must be re-evaluated. If you lose after the hearing, the benefits will be considered an overpayment. However, if you made the request in good faith, you may qualify for waiver, (see Chapter 11).

§ 1010 - Lost or Stolen Checks

If your monthly check has been lost or has been stolen you should report this immediately to the Social Security office. They will issue a stop payment on that check and will reissue a replacement check. Usually you will receive it within 15 days. If you find the lost or stolen check before the replacement check is issued, you can cash the check but you must notify Social Security that you found it. If you receive the replacement check anyway it must be returned. When Social Security puts a stop payment on a check it takes a long time for it to become effective. If you find your missing check within a week or two after you reported it as lost or stolen, you should be able to cash it.

A replacement check will have your Social Security claim number (§1407) on it and will say that it is a substitute check. It will not be dated the third day of the month. It will be dated as of the date it is actually issued.

If the check is not lost or stolen but is only misplaced, Social Security will not make an immediate reissue. They will wait three days after it was issued. Action is taken to immediately replace a lost or stolen check. If your check is stolen or lost you must be able to give some reason why you believe it is stolen or lost instead of misplaced.

§ 1011 - What to Do if Your Check Doesn't Come

The overwhelming majority of the beneficiaries receive their Social Security checks on time each month without experiencing any delays or interruptions, but sometimes there are problems. Each month there are thousands of people across the country who do not receive their checks when due.

As noted in §1002, the first check after you apply for benefits can take anywhere from two weeks to three months and sometimes more. If you do not receive the first check within a month of the time it is due, you should call your Social Security office to find out when you can expect it in the near future or if it will take several more months. Some cases can be processed through the computer system and other cases cannot. The cases that go through the computer system are done faster. If your case is not being handled this way, Social Security will tell you. Expect an additional two or three months for your check to come. If Social Security tells you that the check will come within two months do not call them back the next week and ask where it is. Sometimes you can actually delay the processing of your claim by making too many inquiries. If you have not received your first check within ninety days from the time you gave Social Security all the information and documents they requested, you have a right to an expedited payment. This is discussed in §1013.

After your initial claim is processed your case will be set up on the computer system so that you will receive regular monthly checks automatically. Checks are usually paid on the third day of the month. If your check is received, but is lost or stolen, see §1010. In that case you should notify Social Security immediately. If your check is not received at all, you should wait three mailing days before notifying Social Security. Sometimes delays occur with the Post Office.

If your check does not come when it should, there is no point notifying Social Security before three mailing days have passed. First of all, the Social Security telephone lines and the Social Security district office will be jammed with other people who have not received their checks on time. It will take you a long time to get through to somebody at Social Security in the beginning of the month for this reason. But the most important reason for not notifying Social Security until three mailing days have passed is because Social Security will not do anything anyway. Their procedures require them to wait three mailing days before taking any action to replace the check. If you should finally get through to a district office before the third mailing day after the check is due, they will simply send you a form to complete and mail back to them.

If you have not received the check by the third mailing day steps will be taken to issue a replacement. If your check does not come on the third, do not get upset. In most cases you will receive it within three mailing days. If you do not receive it after that you should notify Social Security of the non-receipt of the check. A sample form is located in Appendix 9. This form can be used to notify Social Security of your missing check. Otherwise you can visit the district office in person, call, or write a letter. The easiest way is to write a letter because the phones and offices will be very busy in the first week of any given month.

If you write a letter you should include certain basic information. Give your complete name, your correct mailing address and your former mailing address if you have had a recent change. You must also indicate the claim number and your beneficiary identification code (§1407). Your notice of non-receipt of a check should identify which monthly check has not been received. You can do this by indicating the day the check was due, such as the September third check, or you can describe it as the month for which the check if payable. For instance, the September third check is payable for the August benefit. To avoid confusion you should indicate the month for which the benefit is payable as well as the date you expected the payment. For example, you should say that it is the September third check for the August benefit. If your checks are directly deposited to your bank account, do not contact Social Security at all. The bank must send paperwork to notify Social Security. If you contact Social Security instead of the bank, they will tell you to contact the bank because a bank officer must sign a form before Social Security can do anything. When you mail a notice of non-receipt of a check, address it to your local district office, attention "Service Unit." The Service Unit in the district office handles non-receipt notice (§105).

After you have sent your notice of non-receipt give it about a week and then call to see if it was received. It will be easier at that time to get through to the district office and they should be able to tell you whether or not they have your notice. It takes about 15 days after the notice of non-receipt is processed by the district office for a replacement check to be issued. If you have not received it within 15 days, you should again contact the Social Security district office. They will tell you when to expect the check. It is important *not* to call them before the time frames they give you. If you call too soon the case may have to be pulled out of its normal processing to answer your question. This can result in even further delay.

If you have not received a regular monthly check within a month and a half after it was due, you have a right to an expedited payment. See §1013.

§ 1012 - Replacement Checks

If you notify Social Security that your check is lost or stolen or that you did not receive it (§1010 and 1011) you will be sent a replacement check. This will be a special check which may arrive at any time of the month and may be dated as of any date. Of course you cannot keep both your regular check and the replacement check. One or the other must be returned if you should receive both. It does not matter which one is returned. You can cash whichever one you receive first. If you keep both checks you will be overpaid and will be required to make a refund. In these cases you are almost never eligible for waiver of repayment.

§ 1013 - Expedited Payments

The Social Security Act puts certain deadlines on the time when checks must be paid to you by Social Security. The rules are different depending on whether it is your first check or a regular monthly payment.

In a case involving your first check after you apply for benefits, you may request an expedited payment if the check has not been paid to you within 90 days after the time you gave all the evidence which was requested by Social Security to support the claim (except in disability cases). Social Security is then required by law to pay you within 15 days of your request. To file the request you should go to your district office and tell them you want the expedited payment. If preferred, you may send a letter. The request must be in writing; you cannot do it over the phone. If you go to the district office, they will prepare a written request for you. If you file your request before the 90 days, Social Security will not act on it until the end of the 90-day period.

Please note that if you have filed your application for benefits before the month you are entitled to payment, the 90 days runs from the date on which the first payment is due, not from the date you submitted your last evidence. For example, if you file in June for benefits beginning with the month of September, the 90-day period begins running from October third (October third is the payment check for the September benefits).

If you are receiving regular monthly benefits, a request for expedited payment may be filed 30 days after the fifteenth day of the month in which the payment was due. For example, if you are receiving regular monthly benefits on the third of each month and you do not receive the check due on September third, you may request an expedited payment if you have not received it within 30 days after September fifteenth. The payment must then be issued to you within 15 days of that request. The request for expedited payment can be filed earlier but it will not be acted upon until after the 30 days runs out.

If you do not receive your check despite your request for expedited payment and you are not satisfied with the explanations you are getting from Social Security, you may wish to contact an elected official. See §1014.

§ 1014 - When to Go to Your Congressman

Sometimes, even with the best efforts of Social Security employees, problems can occur which delay payments. If you have followed the procedures outlined in the above sections, but still have not received your check, an elected official will help push your case. You should contact your United States Congressman or your United States Senator. Each Congressman's office usually has a person who keeps in touch with the Social Security Administration.

When the Social Security office receives an inquiry from a Congressman, they will take steps to make sure that your case is handled as quickly as possible. Social Security will locate your folder and put a special "flag" on it to indicate that there is a Congressional inquiry. This will make sure that the case does not get lost in the shuffle and regular reports will be made to the manager of the Social Security office who in turn will make reports to the Congressman's office. It is important to contact your Congressman *only when all else fails.* If you contact your Congressman too soon it may result in additional delays on your case. This is because the case may have to be pulled out of its normal processing to answer the Congressman's inquiry. Call your Congressman only after you have followed the guidelines in the above sections.

Chapter 11
Overpayments

§ 1101 - Overpayments in General

An overpayment arises when you get more Social Security benefits than you are legally entitled to receive. Each year thousands of people are overpaid benefits. Overpayments occur for many reasons. Sometimes it is Social Security's fault, sometimes it is the beneficiary's fault and sometimes it is a combination of both. Of course, Social Security would like to recover any benefits that were erroneously paid. A major effort is now being undertaken by the Social Security Administration to collect back as much of these overpaid benefits as possible.

However, the law and the Social Security rules allow for "waiver" of repayment of the overpayment. In certain cases a beneficiary who has been overpaid will not be required to make a refund. This chapter will discuss the rules and guidelines Social Security uses when determining whether or not to require a full refund of an overpayment.

§ 1102 - Common Causes of Overpayment

There are two separate categories of overpayments. The most usual one is called a "deduction overpayment." In these cases the beneficiary is legally entitled to benefits but for some other reason, part or all of the benefits should not have been paid. This situation frequently arises when the beneficiary has earnings over the limit for the year, but benefits were paid based on a lower estimate.

Another common cause of overpayments is when a new beneficiary becomes entitled on the same Social Security account. For example, a man dies and leaves his wife and two children. They become entitled to benefits. Several months later a child by a previous marriage applies for benefits on that account. Due to the family maximum provisions (§703.2) an overpayment arises retroactively.

When there are three or more beneficiaries receiving survivor benefits the family maximum is usually met. When the widow and first two children filed and started receiving benefits they were paid on the assumption that there would be only three beneficiaries on the account. When the child by the first marriage applies, his application can be retroactive for up to 6 months. Although the benefits will be refigured for the future and the first two children and widow will receive less, the benefits for the past were higher than they should have been.

Another type of overpayment is called an "entitlement overpayment." This occurs when you file for benefits and Social Security pays them but later discovers that you were never eligible. Any benefits you received are an overpayment.

Sometimes overpayments can occur due to clerical errors. When your benefits are being calculated, they are based on the amount of the earnings. Sometimes a clerical error can occur so that the amount of your earnings are figured at a higher level then they actually were. This means that the amount of your benefit was greater than it should have been and the difference is an overpayment.

§ 1103 - Overpayment Procedures

Once Social Security determines that a person has been overpaid, a decision must be made whether to collect back the overpayment or to waive it. If waived, Social Security will not require repayment. Social Security's guidelines and procedures for waiver of repayment are discussed in §§1104-1109.

If Social Security requires a refund, this can be done in different ways. They may accept a partial refund as a compromise in full settlement (§§1110-1111) or allow for repayment over a period of time (§§1113-1114).

When Social Security determines that you have been overpaid a letter will be sent to you advising you of that fact and the amount of the overpayment. The letter will explain how the overpayment occurred. Social Security will always *request* a full refund of the overpaid amount.

If you disagree that there has been an overpayment or with the amount of the overpayment you may request a reconsideration (see Chapter 13).

In the overpayment letter Social Security says they will start withholding 100% of your monthly benefits until the full amount of overpayment has been recovered. If you request an appeal, a waiver, or some other method of repayment, Social Security will hold up any further processing of the recovery until a decision has been made on your request.

§ 1104 - Waiver of Overpayment

Social Security will not require you to refund an overpayment if certain conditions are met. To be eligible you must be "without fault" in causing the overpayment (§1105) *and* repayment would either be "against equity and good conscience" or it would "defeat the purpose of Title II of the Social Security Act." There are *two* requirements for wavier of repayment. The first is "without fault" and the *second* is *alternative*: either "against equity and good conscience" or "defeat the purpose of Title II." "Without fault" is discussed in §§1105; "against equity and good conscience" is discussed in §§1106; and "defeat the purpose of Title II" is discussed in §§1107.

You must satisfy the "without fault" requirement in *all* cases, and either one of the two alternative requirements. An overpayment may be waived if you are without fault and recovery would be against equity and good conscience *or* you are without fault and recovery would defeat the purpose of Title II.

The purpose of Title II of the Social Security Act is to provide a minimum income for persons who are deprived of income by reason of retirement, death or disability. This requirement may be met if recovery would prevent you from meeting your ordinary and necessary living expenses and you have insufficient assets.

If you are found eligible for waiver, you will not be required to repay the overpayment. The slate will be wiped clean and you will have no obligation for repayment at any time.

If you are not eligible for waiver, you will be required to repay. This can be done by a compromise settlement in a lesser sum (§§1110-1111), by partial payments (§1114) or by deductions from your checks (§1113).

§ 1105 - "Without Fault"

Generally, "without fault" means that you gave all information to the Social Security Administration which was necessary to determine your benefits and that you could not reasonably be expected to know that an overpayment would occur by accepting and cashing a particular check. If you cannot establish that you were without fault in causing an overpayment the recovery of the overpayment can never be waived. "Without fault" is a requirement which must be met in all cases of waiver.

SSA may have been at fault in causing the overpayment; nevertheless, *you* must establish that *you* were without fault. SSA's fault does not excuse yours.

Each particular case will be examined to determine its own specific facts. The general principles are that the beneficiary must report everything which may affect payment of benefits and must exercise a high degree of care when determining whether or not a check is payable.

There are many situations which have occurred repeatedly involving the question of whether or not a beneficiary was at fault in causing an overpayment. SSA has identified certain situations where it is presumed that the beneficiary was without fault in the absence of other information which indicates otherwise. These situations are described in §1105.

There are some situations where SSA presumes the beneficiary was at fault. The most obvious case is when duplicate payments have been made. If you cash your regular monthly check *and* a replacement check, you will not be considered without fault. If you file an application for benefits but you are already receiving on another account, you are at fault if you accept benefits from both accounts, unless you told SSA that you were already entitled on the first account.

You are at fault in causing an overpayment if you do not exercise a high degree of care about your monthly benefits. If for example, you return to work but do not report this, you will be at fault if an overpayment results.

If you do not deal in good faith, you will not be held to be without fault. For example, if you incurred an overpayment in one year because of work, requested and obtained a waiver of repayment but then worked again in the following year, you will not be considered without fault for the second year because you knew that your earnings would affect your benefits.

If you withhold information from SSA which could affect your benefits, you will not be without fault. At the time you filed your application, you are given a receipt which lists on it the things which must be reported. From time to time SSA puts "stuffers" into check envelopes to remind you of things to report.

Examples of "Without Fault"

Over the years SSA has become aware of certain typical situations where the overpaid person is without fault. They have identified these situations and will assume that if your case fits within these facts you are "without fault" in causing the overpayment. This assumption may be overcome by other facts which show bad faith or failure to exercise a high degree of care about your monthly benefits.

Situation One

A person is usually found to be without fault if there is a mistake about the benefit rates. SSA will not require you to know the exact amount of your monthly benefits but if the error is so grossly disproportionate to what your payment should be, you may be at fault. For example, John applied for retirement benefits and was told he would receive $600.00 per month. The first check was $600.00, but the second check was $6,000.00. This payment is so out of line with what he should have expected, that he may be at fault unless he attempted to verify it with SSA. If he received checks in the amount of $620.00 all along after he retired and then was advised a year later that the correct amount should have been only $600, Social Security will consider him to be without fault in causing the overpayment because he cannot be expected to calculate the exact benefit amount.

Situation Two

If you file for monthly benefits and you are told that you have earned enough to be eligible but it later turns out you did not, you will be considered without fault in causing any overpayment (unless your earnings record was fraudulent).

Situation Three

If you believed that only the *net* amount of your paycheck counted towards the retirement test, you may be without fault in causing an overpayment. If your earnings for a year are over a certain level it will cause a reduction in your benefits. The gross amount of earnings, before taxes are deducted, is what counts. Many times a beneficiary believes that only his take home pay is counted for the annual earnings limitation or the monthly limit. Your "take home" pay is the amount of your paycheck after all deductions, such as income tax, union dues, insurance, hospitalization, etc. If your net cash earnings (take home pay) for the year is below the annual earnings limit, then Social Security will generally consider you to be "without fault" if you believed that only your take home pay counted. If your net cash earnings is over the limit for the year, SSA will consider whether or not you reported the net amount or the gross amount for purposes of the annual earnings limitations. If you report the amount of take home pay to SSA this will indicate that you understood that only the take home pay counted and not the gross pay. Social Security will want to look at your pay stubs to determine the net amount of your take home pay. If you cannot obtain them, they will usually contact your employer to find this out.

Situation Four

You will be considered to be without fault in causing an overpayment if you relied on incorrect information from an official source. An "official source" means SSA or another government agency which you reasonably thought was connected with the administration of social security, such as the Railroad Retirement Board. *Misunderstanding* of correctly given information does not count as misinformation for these purposes.

If you claim misinformation was given to you, Social Security will question you very closely to determine whether of not you misunderstood correct information or whether misinformation was in fact given. They will look to determine your normal understanding, because some people can understand technical requirements better than others. You must give a full explanation of your reliance on wrong information. They will ask for an explanation for your own words. The explanation will have to show what information was received, the time and place it was received, the identity, if possible, of the person who gave the incorrect information and any and all other facts about it. SSA will seek to verify the statements you give by contacting people within the district office or elsewhere who you say gave you the misinformation. If supporting evidence cannot be obtained, the manager or supervisor in the office will make a report as to the likelihood of misinformation being given. If records are no longer available and there is no way to verify your allegations, they will resolve the doubt about it in your favor.

Situation Five

If an overpayment results because a short taxable year for the beneficiary was caused by his death, Social Security will waive any overpayment if there was evidence that the deceased beneficiary intended to limit his yearly earnings to the annual earnings limitations in effect for the year of death. If he dies before December of the year, the annual earnings limit is prorated according to the number of months the beneficiary was alive (§810). For example, if the beneficiary died in the month of June the earnings limitation would be one-half of the annual limit for the year. If the beneficiary had earned under the annual limit up to the time he died and did not intend to earn over the regular limit for the year, the overpayment resulting from the excess earnings will usually be waived. Recovery in this case is deemed to be against equity and good conscience.

Situation Six

Sometimes a person is overpaid because he has earned over the allowable earnings limit for a particular year without realizing that his earnings before he became entitled to benefits in that year would count. For example, you start receiving benefits in June. Your earnings for June through December are only $3,000, well below the annual earnings limit. But you also worked from January through May and earned $10,000. The *total* yearly earnings are $13,000 and will cause deductions for any month you earned over the monthly limit (§804). If you received all your monthly benefits and earned over the monthly limit in all months, you are overpaid. If you believed that your earnings before you became entitled to benefits did not count for the earnings test, Social Security will consider you to be without fault in causing the overpayment. For this rule to apply your earnings for the year beginning with the time you become eligible must not exceed the annual earnings limit for that year. The intent of this rule is to provide for a "without fault" finding if you restrict your earnings to the yearly limit beginning with the time you become eligible for benefits. Although all your earnings for the year are included for purposes of the work test, if you were unaware of this and believed in good faith that only your earnings after entitlement counted, Social Security may find you to be without fault.

If you are an employee and your wages in the deduction months (months which are subject to withholding because of earnings) did not exceed the total monthly benefit for that month, recovery of the overpayment is deemed inequitable. In this situation the overpayment may be waived without considering your financial circumstances. The following example shows the application of these rules.

Example: William began his entitlement to retirement benefits in March 1994. His monthly amount was established at $900. He earned $4,000 in the months of January and February. His wife also became entitled to wife's benefits in the amount of $450. Benefit checks were issued to Mr. Smith and his wife each month beginning with March 1994 based on his statement that he would not earn over the yearly amount permitted under the law. Mr. Smith's employer later reported wage of $15,160 in 1994. It seems that Mr. Smith misunderstood the retirement test. Mr. Smith believed that he could earn $11,160 after qualifying for benefits and reduced his hours of work so his earnings would not exceed $11,160 ($1,160 a month for ten months). On the basis of his earnings, he and his wife were overpaid. Mr. Smith is without fault in incurring the overpayment and recovery is deemed to be against equity and good conscience because the earnings in each of the months affected by the potential deductions (March and April) are less than his monthly benefit amount for those months.

The term "eligibility" for benefits is used broadly for purposes of this rule. It does not necessarily mean legal entitlement. It will usually mean what the beneficiary understands. If the beneficiary believes that his earnings before he files his application do not count, Social Security will look at it from that view. If he believes his earnings before reaching retirement age won't count, they will apply the rule that way.

Situation Seven

If your earnings for a year go over what you expected them to be, you may be found to be without fault in causing a resulting overpayment if the reason the earnings are greater is one of the following: 1 - You received a retroactive increase in pay; 2 - Your rate of pay was higher than you realized; 3 - You made an agreement with your employer that your earnings would be kept below a certain limit but the employer did not restrict the earnings and you were unable to keep accurate records; 4 - There were five pay days in a month and you only expected four pay days, (if your monthly earnings with only four pay days would be under the monthly limit), or you figured your annual earnings based on four pay days per month and you would have been under the yearly limit on that basis.

Situation Eight

You may be without fault in causing an overpayment if Social Security continued to send you checks after you notified them that you returned to work, or about something else which should have caused a deduction. You qualify under this rule if you believe in good faith that you are entitled to receive the checks because Social Security is still sending them to you. SSA will want to know how and when you gave notice of the events that were reported and what your reaction was to the continued payment of monthly checks.

Many times a person will say that notice of the deduction event (such as return to work or not having a child in your care) was to be given by a relative or friend. If this is the case, Social Security will not consider you without fault because *you* have the duty to report these events, *not* someone else. However, if you routinely rely on this other person to report these things for you, Social Security may take that as a circumstance to consider. For instance, if you are housebound or unable to speak English and your daughter or son takes care of your affairs, Social Security may allow that as a reasonable excuse.

Situation Nine

Sometimes overpayments occur because employees receive special types of payments which they do not realize are included in annual earnings for purposes of the retirement test. If you believe in good faith that a bonus, vacation pay, traveling expense or other similar payment was not to be included in figuring your earnings, Social Security may consider you to be without fault in causing an overpayment which was caused by the inclusion of those payments. Social Security will contact your employer to determine the amount and the type of special payment involved. If you were unaware that those special payments counted, Social Security will generally consider you to be without fault in causing an overpayment resulting from that extra pay. Please note that you must still satisfy the second part of the waiver test (§1104).

Situation Ten

Another common situation causing overpayments is when the beneficiary is confused with regard to how the annual earnings test works. An overpaid beneficiary sometimes believes that earnings over the limit for the taxable year cause deductions from your checks only for months beginning with the first month in which your earnings go over. If you report timely to Social Security that your earnings reached that level when they did, you may be eligible for a waiver if you are overpaid. Two important factors are considered: 1 - did you in fact notify SSA when your earnings reached the yearly amount or immediately thereafter, and 2 - if so waiver can apply only for months *before* the time you reported your earnings. You know your earnings *after* you go over the limit will affect your benefit, so you cannot be without fault if you accept them.

Situation Eleven

If you receive benefits as a dependent on the account of a retired worker, your benefits may be subject to deductions if the worker earns over the annual limit (§801). If you were overpaid as a result, you may be "without fault" if you didn't know (and had no reason to know) that the worker's earnings would go over the limit, *and* you were not living with the worker. You must still meet the second part of the waiver rules (§1104).

Situation Twelve

If your benefits end during a year, your earnings after termination nevertheless are counted for the work test. This may result in overpayment of benefits which were paid. If you believed that your earnings after termination of entitlement would not cause deductions for the earlier months, you may be "without fault" in causing the overpayment. You must still meet the second part of the waiver rules (§1104).

Social Security will require a breakdown of your earnings to see if you earned over the yearly limit during the time you were entitled. They will require evidence of the earnings, such as pay stubs or a letter from your employer.

Situation Thirteen

You may be "without fault" in causing an overpayment if you made a good faith effort to restrict your earnings, but you misunderstood the retirement test or there was some other unusual circumstance.

Examples:

- A self-employed person believed the monthly wage limits applied instead of the "substantial services" rule (§804).

- You wanted to restrict your earnings and kept an ongoing record, but you made an arithmetical error, or you lost a pay slip.

- You believed you could earn up to the yearly limit beginning with the month of your first check up until the end of the year.

- You believed you could earn the yearly limit for a 12 month period which began with the first month you are eligible, for example 3/1/94 through 3/1/95, rather than a calendar year.

Social Security will require verification of what you say, such as evidence of your wages for specific periods.

§ 1106 - "Against Equity and Good Conscience"

One of the alternatives to the second part of the waiver rules (§1104) is that recovery of the overpayment (making you pay it back) would be against equity and good conscience. This occurs if, relying on payment of benefits, you gave up a valuable right, or changed your position for the worse. If you claim waiver because of this, Social Security will require you to give a full explanation of the circumstances. They will require verification of what you say. The evidence required will depend on the facts of your particular case. See the next section for some examples.

Remember that in all cases you must establish "without fault" (§1105). If you cannot establish "against equity and good conscience," you may still be eligible for waiver if you can establish that recovery would "defeat the purpose of Title II" (§1107).

Examples of "Against Equity and Good Conscience"

Whether your case will be considered to meet the "against equity" requirement depends on the particular facts. Here are some examples of situations where the requirement is satisfied.

Example: John applied for retirement benefits and was awarded. He resigned from his job, relying on the monthly benefits. Three years later it is discovered that his earnings record was wrong, without fault on John's part. He does not have the required insured status (§601) and therefore he has been overpaid. Because of his age, he cannot get another job. Recovery of the overpayment would be against equity and good conscience.

Example: Agnes is a widow who applies for and receives survivor benefits. Counting on this income, she enters her daughter in college, which would not otherwise be possible. It turns out that her husband didn't work long enough and Agnes is therefore overpaid. Recovery of the overpayment would be inequitable.

Other Situations

In certain situations you are considered to be "without fault" in causing an overpayment (§1105). In some of these same cases, recovery is also considered to be "against equity and good conscience" and you are therefore eligible for waiver of the overpayment. If so you do not have to establish financial hardship.

Certain "without fault" situations are described in §1105. Situations three, four and five of that section are also considered to meet the "against equity" rule. Situation six also meets the rule *if* you are an employee and your wages in months subject to deductions are less than the total monthly benefits for those months. This is discussed more fully in §1105, Situation Six.

§ 1107 - "Defeat the Purpose of Title II"

An alternative requirement of the second part of the waiver rules (§1104) is that recovery of overpayment would "defeat the purpose of Title II of the Social Security Act." This is the law which provides for social security benefits. Its purpose is to keep the disabled, the retired and survivors out of destitution. You meet the "defeat the purpose" requirement if recovery of the overpayment would deprive you of funds which are necessary for your support.

Social Security looks first at your income (from all sources) and your ordinary and necessary living expenses (§1109). If you do not need all your income, then Social Security will look at your assets. If they are below certain levels, you will not have to repay the overpayment (§1108).

If you do not meet the "defeat the purpose" requirement, you may be eligible for waiver if recovery would be "against equity and good conscience" (§1106). In all cases, you must also be "without fault" for waiver to be approved (§1104).

Examples of "Defeat the Purposes of Title II"

Example 1: Virginia was overpaid $900.00. She had income of $195.00 from a private pension and $430.00 in Social Security benefits. She lives alone and has no dependents. Virginia listed current monthly expenses of $620.00 which included $275.00 rent for her apartment, $20.00 for clothes, $200.00 for food, $30.00 for medical care and prescriptions, $10.00 for church contributions, $30.00 for utilities, and $55.00 for auto maintenance and insurance. She submitted bills verifying her rent, utilities, prescriptions, and automobile insurance. Since the overall expenses seem reasonable and necessary for ordinary living expenses, a finding of "defeat the purpose of Title II" would be justified.

Example 2: Dan was overpaid $350.00. He and his wife live in a small home valued at $50,000.00. They also own a motor boat valued at $7,000.00 and on which they still owe $4,000.00. Their only income is Social Security benefits of $600.00. They only have $200.00 in a savings account.

They state that their monthly expenses are $640.00 including $100.00 for property taxes, $300.00 for food, $20.00 for clothing, $20.00 for prescriptions, $50.00 for utilities, $50.00 for insurance and upkeep of their car, and $100.00 to repay the loan and to maintain their boat. As the boat is not a necessity and their expenses for ordinary living costs do not approach their income, a finding of "defeat the purpose of Title II" would *not* be justified.

Example 3: Will, his wife Mae, and son Joe have $500.00 in the bank. Will lives in a low income housing project and alleges that his total monthly expenses are only $400.00, consisting of rent of $80.00, food of $300.00, and telephone of $20.00. His income is only $380.00. His expenses can be presumed to be reasonable. A finding of "defeat the purpose of Title II" is justified. If, however, his monthly income were $450.00, "defeat the purpose of Title II" would not be justified.

Example 4: Joe was overpaid $600.00 because it was determined that he did not have enough work to collect Social Security benefits. He has no monthly income. He does have $5,000.00 in the bank. He has outstanding medical bills of $2,200.00 and more medical bills are coming in monthly. The medical bills will soon wipe out his assets. In this case, even though his assets exceed the limit, a decision that recovery of the overpayment would "defeat the purpose of Title II" would be justified.

Example 5: Charlie and Maureen were overpaid $1,600.00. They have $5,900.00 in a savings account. Their only income is Social Security of $600.00. Their monthly expenses are $600.00. A split decision can be made on this overpayment. Social Security can recover $900.00 to reduce their total assets to $5,000.00. The remaining $700.00 overpayment can be waived because reducing their assets below $5,000.00 will "defeat the purpose of Title II."

Example 6: Bob and Dale were notified that they were overpaid $500.00. They claimed that they were without fault in causing the overpayment and unable to repay. Social Security learned that they still have the $500.00 in Social Security benefits deposited in a savings account. Recovery of the overpayment would *not* "defeat the purpose of Title II." However, if they had used $300.00 to pay debts, this portion of the overpayment may justify the finding of "defeat the purpose of Title II." They will still be responsible to repay the remaining $200.00.

§ 1108 - Guidelines on Assets

If all your income is required for your support (§1109), Social Security will look at your assets to decide if recovery of an overpayment would "defeat the purpose of Title II" (§1107).

Generally, Social Security will not require you to reduce your assets below $3,000 to pay back an overpayment. If you have a dependent, the guideline is $5,000. You can allow an additional $600 for each additional dependent. For instance, the guideline for a person with two dependents is $5,600.

Example: you are overpaid $2,500. You are "without fault" and you need all your income for your support. You have no dependent, but your assets are $4,000. Social Security will waive recovery of $1,500, but require repayment of $1,000, the amount by which your assets exceed the guidelines.

Social Security has some flexibility with these guidelines, depending on the circumstances.

Example: Harry has assets over the guidelines. However, his wife is seriously ill. There are outstanding medical bills which, when paid, will reduce the assets below $5,000. More medical bills are anticipated which will soon wipe out the remaining assets. Harry's present assets will *not* preclude a finding of "defeat the purpose of Title II."

"Assets" include all liquid assets, such as bank accounts, stocks, bonds, etc., and the reasonable value of non-liquid assets such as real estate. Social Security does not include household furnishings, clothes, the family car, or a home of reasonable value. Income-producing real estate is not included because the income from it is considered in evaluating your income and expenses (§1109). Social Security does include assets resulting from a pending inheritance, even if not yet received. If you are a beneficiary of a trust fund, the amount in the fund is also included, even if not immediately available.

§ 1109 - Guidelines on Income and Expenses

To be eligible for waiver of an overpayment on the ground that recovery would "defeat the purpose of Title II" (§1107), you first must show that you need all of your income to meet your living expenses. Social Security has flexibility when considering your income and expenses. They do not wish to significantly lower your standard of living if this would cause a hardship. However, they will not accept expenditures which are beyond the ordinary and necessary living expenses for food, clothing and shelter.

Income from all sources is counted, including the income of a spouse and other dependent relatives living in the same house, whether or not they receive benefits.

The amount of reasonable expenses depends on the cost-of-living for your area. The knowledge and judgment of the local Social Security employee reviewing your case is considered. Expenses include those incurred for food, clothing, rent, mortgage payments, utilities, maintenance, life, accident and health insurance premiums, taxes, installment payments, medical and drug bills, child support, charitable contributions, newspapers, cigarettes, household supplies, gasoline and other miscellaneous expenses.

Expenses to purchase or maintain non-essential items such as a boat or vacation home are not counted.

If a debt will be paid off in the near future, this will also be considered.

If your allegations about your living expenses, income or assets appear incorrect, Social Security will require you to produce evidence to prove them. They also require verification in the following situations:

1. Expenses are over $500 per month, plus $100 for each dependent.

2. Expenses appear too high, even if lower than in (1) above.

3. The Social Security interviewer doubts that the income and assets of other household members have been included.

4. You received a large retroactive check which was an overpayment and you claim you no longer have the funds because of unusually large expenditures.

If your expenses are higher than your income, Social Security will want to know how you meet them. If you cannot produce evidence of this, such as a dwindling bank account, they will not believe you.

If your monthly expenses are less than $100 plus $75 for each dependent, Social Security will presume they are reasonable and necessary.

These are no hard and fast rules about the types of acceptable evidence. If evidence you first submit appears convincing, you will not be required to produce better evidence which may be available. Examples of evidence commonly accepted are letters from employers, copies of tax returns, tax receipts and bills, installment payment books, etc.

§ 1110 - The Compromise Settlement

The Social Security Administration has authority to accept compromise settlements where the amount of the overpayment is not greater than $20,000. This means that they may accept less than the total overpayment in full settlement. In that case there will be no further recovery of the balance. An offer to settle an overpayment greater than $20,000 will be referred to the Justice Department or the General Accounting Office.

Social Security cannot compromise an overpayment claim if the overpayment resulted from fraud, unless the overpaid person is deceased and the overpayment is $5,000 or less. However, if someone else who is still alive contributed to the fraud, the claim cannot be compromised regardless of the amount.

A claim to recover an overpayment may be compromised only if one of the following conditions exist:

1. You are unable to repay the full amount within a reasonable time or the Government is unable to enforce collection within a reasonable time; or

2. There is real doubt about the Government's ability to prove its case in court; or

3. The cost of collecting the claim is likely to exceed the amount of recovery (this is presumed if the difference between the compromise offer and the amount of the overpayment is less than $500.00).

A compromise offer must be in writing and signed by the overpaid person. An offer signed by an attorney may also be accepted if it appears he is in a position to carry out its terms.

The written statement should include:

1. The reason a lesser amount has been offered.

2. The overpaid person's name, claim number (§1407), and current address.

3. The total amount of overpayment.

4. The amount offered as a compromise.

5. When and how the compromise amount will be refunded. (It should be within 30 days after acceptance of the offer.)

6. An understanding that if the compromise is not timely paid, the full amount will be due.

Once the offer is made, it will take several months to get an answer. The decision whether to accept it is not made in the District Office. It is referred to a Program Service Center or the Office of Disability Operations (§102). If Social Security does not accept the offer, they may make a counter offer.

Guidelines for Accepting Compromise Offers

Social Security will first decide if they have authority to compromise (§1110). If so, they will consider whether they could recover the overpayment by withholding checks within the next three months. If so the offer to settle should be at least 80% of the total overpayment.

If enforced collection is not possible, an offer of 50% of the overpayment will usually be accepted if you are financially unable to repay in full. An offer of less than 50% may be accepted if you are financially unable to pay more than the amount offered.

If you are financially able to repay in full, but enforced collection is not possible, an offer of 60% will usually be accepted.

These guidelines are simply that; they are not binding rules. Social Security has discretion to accept or reject any compromise offer. There are no appeal rights from a rejection of an offer to compromise.

If a request for waiver of overpayment (§1104) or an appeal from the overpayment determination is pending, no action will be taken on the compromise offer until the outcome.

§ 1111 - Repayment

If you are not eligible for waiver of an overpayment (§1104), and there is no compromise settlement (§1110), the overpayment must be repaid. When Social Security notifies you that you are overpaid, they demand repayment in full.

If you are a beneficiary, they will tell you that your checks will be withheld until the overpayment is recovered in full.

Nevertheless, Social Security will accept installments (§1114) or impose only partial monthly deductions (§1113) if you ask them to do this.

No interest is charged on overpayments, no matter how long you take to repay.

§ 1112 - Deductions

Social Security may withhold your monthly benefits to recover an overpayment. They always propose to withhold benefits in full until the total amount is recovered. If you ask, however, they will usually agree to withhold only part of the monthly benefits. They will do this provided that the full overpayment will be recovered within 12 months, and the partial withholding is at least $10 per month.

If recovery by partial withholding for 12 months would cause a financial hardship, Social Security may extend the period, but no longer than 36 months. They will require financial information from you to explain the hardship. Interest is never charged on past due amounts.

§ 1113 - Installments

Social Security will accept repayment of an overpayment in monthly installments instead of deductions from your checks, if you ask for this arrangement. The same rules which apply to partial monthly deductions (§1112) also apply to installments.

Chapter 12
Medicare

§ 1201 - Medicare in General

Medicare is the health insurance program under the auspices of the Health Care Financing Administration, a branch of the Department of Health and Human Services. Medicare is no longer technically under the jurisdiction of the Social Security Administration, although SSA is a primary source of information, applications and claims for Medicare. All questions on Medicare can be answered by contacting any Social Security office, or a toll-free number - 1-800-638-6833.

Medicare is divided into two parts: Hospital Insurance (sometimes referred to as "Part A"), and Medical Insurance (sometimes referred to as "Part B").

Hospital Insurance is financed through a portion of the FICA payroll deduction from the paychecks of workers. Medical Insurance is partially financed through the collection of monthly premiums. These are either deducted from Social Security checks or paid directly by covered individuals. See Appendix 12 for the amount of the premiums.

§ 1202 - Hospital Insurance

Hospital insurance pays for four basic areas of medical care: in-patient care in a hospital; medically necessary in-patient care in a skilled nursing facility immediately following hospitalization (most nursing homes are not skilled nursing facilities); home health care; and hospice care.

All hospital insurance claims are paid on the basis of benefit periods. The first benefit period begins with the first hospitalization, but ends 60 calendar days after the termination of medicare services (hospitalization, a skilled nursing facility or rehabilitation services). There is no limit to the number of benefit periods an individual can have under hospital insurance.

Medicare hospital insurance does not pay for the entire stay in the hospital. In each benefit period, Medicare pays for all covered services for the first through the sixtieth day, except for the average cost of one day's hospitalization. For the sixty-first through ninetieth day in the hospital, Medicare pays for all covered services except for one-quarter of the average cost of *each* day in the hospital. In addition, every Medicare beneficiary is entitled to 60 life-time reserve days. For life-time reserve days, Medicare pays for all covered services except for the cost of one half of the average cost for *each* day in the hospital. See Appendix 12 for these co-payment amounts.

§ 1203 - Medical Insurance

Medicare medical insurance pays for six basic areas of medical care:

1. Doctor's services, both in his office and in the hospital.

2. Out-patient hospital care.

3. Out-patient physical and speech therapy.

4. Home health care.

5. Ambulances.

6. Medically necessary durable medical equipment, such as wheel-chairs.

All payments under Medicare Part B are based on reasonable charges, not the current charges made by the physicians. Reasonable charges are determined by comparing the customary charge made by each doctor in the previous calendar year for each service with the "prevailing rate" for each service. The prevailing rate is the amount which will cover the customary charge in seventy-five percent of the bills submitted to medicare in the previous year.

Medicare medical insurance pays eighty percent of the reasonable charge, after a predetermined deductible has been met, based on covered services, i.e., what Medicare would have paid which may be different from the doctor's fee. All deductibles for Medicare Part B are based on the calendar year.

Premiums

You must pay a monthly premium for Medical Insurance, see Appendix 12 for the amount. If you do not elect to be covered by Medical Insurance when you are first eligible, you can enroll only during a General Enrollment Period (see §407). If more than 12 months have passed since the close of your Initial Enrollment Period, you must pay an extra 10% for each full 12 month period beginning with the first month after the Initial Enrollment Period and ending with the last month of the General Enrollment Period in which you apply.

Example: John became 65 and otherwise eligible for Medical Insurance in January, 1992, but he did not enroll for Part B until January 15, 1992, during a General Enrollment Period. His Initial Enrollment Period closed April, 1992, the third month after his 65th birthday (see §407). The months considered for the premium increase are May 1992 through March, 1994. There are 23 months in this period, which is only one full 12 month period. His monthly premium will be increased by 10% (rounded to the nearest 10 cents).

For purposes of figuring the extra premium, you do *not* count any months during which you were covered *both* by Hospital Insurance (Part A) *and* an employer group health plan (§1204).

§ 1204 - Private Health Insurance

Medicare is designed to provide basic protection against the very high cost of health care, but it will never pay all of your medical expenses. Because of this, many private insurance companies offer different protection in their policies. You should shop and compare different companies to determine which policy would be best for you.

For example, if you have need for several prescriptions, perhaps a company which covers prescription costs would be more advantageous. Other plans may offer eyeglass or dental plans. There is no one supplemental health plan which is best for everybody.

If you are over age 65 and you (or your spouse) work for an employer who has 20 or more employees, your employer is required to offer you the same health insurance benefits that he is offering to his young workers. If you continue working after 65 you have a choice of either accepting or rejecting your employer's health plan. If you accept it, Medicare will become a secondary health insurance plan for you; your employer's health plan would be the primary insurance plan (the first payer). If you drop Part B because you are covered by the private plan, you may re-enroll when the private coverage ends, see §407.

You have the option of rejecting your employer's health plan and if you do, Medicare will become the primary health insurance plan.

§ 1205 - What is Not Covered

Medicare hospital insurance pays for all routine care in a hospital, including semi-private room, all your meals and regular nursing service, lab tests and X-rays. It does not cover other items which are purely for personal convenience, such as the television, a radio, or a telephone. It will not pay the charge for private duty nurses or extra charges for a private room unless it is determined to be medically necessary, for example, to isolate a contagious disease.

Medicare medical insurance will not pay for the following services:

1. Routine physical examinations and tests related to routine physical examination.

2. Routine foot care.

3. Eye or hearing examinations for prescribing or fitting eyeglasses or hearing aids (Medicare will pay for some eye services related to cataract surgery).

4. Immunizations.

5. Most cosmetic surgery.

6. Most dental care, (dental care will be covered only if it involves surgery of the jaw or the setting of fractures of the jaw, or facial bones).

The above sections are by no means a comprehensive list of what is or is not covered by Medicare. For more complete information you may obtain a copy of the Medicare Handbook published by Social Security.

§ 1206 - Assignment of Benefits

Assignment of benefits is a procedure by which the doctor agrees to accept direct payment from Medicare for services he provided to you. If a doctor accepts an assignment, he agrees to accept the amount that Medicare approves as his full charge for the service. Medicare would then pay eighty percent of that amount. You are still responsible to pay the twenty percent that Medicare does not pay.

§ 1207 - When to File Claims

Virtually all services rendered by hospitals and skilled nursing facilities are submitted directly to Medicare by the hospital. They will receive payment directly. You will receive only a notice of how much was paid and what the covered services are.

Some physicians, whether or not they accept assignment, will forward the claim for reimbursement to Medicare. If the physician does forward the claim to Medicare and has accepted assignment, you will receive an explanation of how much money was paid to the physician.

If the physician does not accept assignment, you will receive an explanation of how much Medicare pays along with a check.

You may forward your bills to Medicare as soon as you receive them, or you may save and submit them all at once. Since many people have a tendency to save their bills until the deductible is met or to save up their bills for the entire year and submit them all at once, the last three months of the year and the first three months of the year are very busy for Medicare and may result in a substantially longer time to process your request for reimbursement.

It is generally advisable to submit your Medicare claims on a "flow" basis. As soon as you receive the service, submit the bill.

§ 1208 - Processing of Claims

Claims for Medicare medical insurance benefits are not processed by either the Social Security Administration or the Health Care Financing Administration. These are processed by various private health insurance companies throughout the country. These companies are known as Medicare carriers. For example, all Medicare Part B claims for services provided by doctors in Alabama will be forwarded to Medicare Blue Cross/Blue Shield of Alabama in Birmingham. Claims in the State of Hawaii are sent to Medicare Aetna Life and Casualty Company in Honolulu. You are told who your carrier is when you become entitled to Medicare.

If you do forward the Medicare claim to the wrong office, that office will forward it to the correct one.

§ 1209 - The Medicare Card

Everyone entitled to Medicare hospital insurance or medical insurance is issued a red-white-and-blue card which is entitled "Health Insurance Social Security Act." This is known as the "Medicare card." The information on the card includes your name, your Social Security claim number and your sex. It indicates whether you are entitled to hospital insurance benefits only, medical insurance benefits only, or both. It also shows the effective date.

You are issued only one Medicare card which is good for as long as you are entitled. Social Security will issue replacements only if your card is lost or stolen. It normally takes about four to six weeks after your initial application for Medicare is processed to receive the card. If you need to use Medicare before you receive it, the Social Security office can issue you a temporary letter of eligibility which will contain the information on the Medicare card. This can be used instead by the doctors and hospitals.

Chapter 13
Appeals

§ 1301 - Appeals in General

Social Security regulations establish an appeals process which must be followed if you wish to appeal a decision in your case. Not every administrative action may be appealed (§1302). The appeals process has different levels; the reconsideration, the hearing, and the Appeals Council review. You must go through this process before a federal court will review your case.

You have the right to be represented by an attorney at any stage in your dealings with the Social Security Administration. This is not usually necessary unless you have a problem. You should be represented if you go to the hearing stage of the appeals process. An attorney may charge you a fee, if the amount has been approved by SSA (§1310).

The legal rules of evidence do not apply in these administrative proceedings. This means you may submit any evidence you wish, even if it is not admissible in a court of law.

§ 1302 - What You Can and Cannot Appeal

You can appeal only an "initial determination." This is a formal decision affecting benefits, a period of disability, your earnings record, or *entitlement* to Medicare. Claims for payment under medical insurance (Medicare Part B) are not reviewed by the Social Security Administration. Disputes about such payments are reviewed by the insurance company which administers medical insurance in your state. These cases cannot be reviewed in federal court.

Initial determinations include: awards or disallowances of monthly benefit claims; computations and recomputations of monthly benefit amounts; decisions on deductions from benefits and termination of benefits; "representative payee" (§1414) determinations; overpayment decisions; and determinations about your earnings record.

Whenever an initial determination is made concerning your case, you will receive a written notice. This may be an award certificate, a disallowance letter, or a letter explaining the decision. The date of this letter starts the time limit for a request for a reconsideration (§1308).

Administrative decisions which are *not* initial determinations include: payment of combined checks (§1004); withholding of part of a monthly benefit to recover an overpayment; and authorizing the amount of an attorney's fee. Any administrative action which is not an initial determination cannot be appealed through the normal appeals process, and is not reviewable in court.

§ 1303 - The Reconsideration

The first step in the administrative appeals process is the reconsideration. You or your representative, such as an attorney, may request it. The request may also be filed by another person whose benefit rights are adversely affected by a determination made in your case.

You do not have to fill out the forms yourself. The Claims Representative (§105) will do this for you, but you or your representative must sign them.

If you are appealing a disability denial, you should bring with you the names and addresses of all your treating doctors and hospitals. Be prepared to describe in detail any change in your condition, and how it affects your daily activities.

You may submit any evidence you wish. Copies of medical reports and hospital records will be accepted, unless they appear to be altered.

The reconsideration is a review of your record by a member of a different staff from the one that made the initial determination. You do not usually have the right to appear in person, although an experimental project is being conducted in certain parts of the country which allows you to be present and give testimony. In overpayment cases you may appear for a personal conference instead of the usual reconsideration (§1304).

The request for a reconsideration must be filed within 60 days of the notice of the initial determination (§1308).

§ 1304 - The Personal Conference - Overpayment Cases

If your appeal is from a denial of your request for waiver of an overpayment (see Chapter 11), you may have a personal conference instead of a reconsideration. The personal conference is usually conducted by a Claims Representative (§105) at your local District Office. You may appear (with an attorney if you wish) and explain your case. Any evidence you wish to submit will be considered.

The personal conference must be requested within 60 days of the notice of the initial determination (§1308).

§ 1305 - The Hearing

The hearing is the single most important step in the appeals process. It is conducted by an Administrative Law Judge (ALJ). The ALJ will independently review your case on the basis of the evidence in the file, any evidence you submit, and your sworn testimony.

You may appear in person and be represented by an attorney. The proceedings will be recorded on a tape recorder, not by a stenographer. A hearing assistant may be present to operate the recording system.

The administrative law judge may arrange for the testimony of expert witnesses called on behalf of the government. Vocational experts are frequently utilized in disability cases. You may produce your own experts to testify, but you are responsible for any fee. You may also request the ALJ to issue subpoenas requiring the attendance and testimony of witnesses or the production of documents or other evidence. Any such request for subpoenas should be made as far in advance of the hearing as possible (and no less than five days).

Notice of the time and place of the hearing is sent to you at least 10 days in advance. If you have a lawyer, call him as soon as you receive your notice to make sure he received one.

In disability cases it is very important for you to appear in person. The judge will ask you about your limitations, your medical treatments and medications, your work background and your daily activities, among other things.

You must be fully prepared to answer these questions. We cannot discuss all the questions you may be asked, but your lawyer will go over them with you before the hearing.

Be as specific and complete as possible in your answers, but *never exaggerate.* The judge will be looking for this. You should be able to describe how much weight, in pounds, you are able to lift and carry, how long you can sit, stand and walk, and whether you have limitations bending, climbing, pushing or pulling.

If you suffer from pain, be prepared to describe it as sharp or dull, its frequency and location, what activities produce or aggravate it, and what relieves it. You should describe any side effects from medication, such as drowsiness, nausea, or impaired concentration.

The hearing will last about an hour in the usual case. If you wish to submit additional evidence you may request the judge to hold the record open for a week or two.

The judge will make a written decision on your case within a month after the hearing. If you win, you will receive benefits about a month later.

The request for hearing must be filed within 60 days of the reconsideration denial (§1308). Your hearing will be scheduled within two or three months.

§ 1306 - Appeals Council Review

You may request review of the administrative law judge's decision within 60 days. The Appeals Council may also review the decision of its own initiative within the same time.

The Appeals Council may deny your request for review, which it does in most cases. If so, the decision of the administrative law judge is the final decision of SSA.

If the Appeals Council believes that a significant question of law or policy is involved in your case, it may grant review. In some cases it may allow you or your lawyer to appear before it in Washington, D.C., and present oral arguments. The Appeals Council then will make its decision, which is final.

Sometimes cases are referred back to the administrative law judge to obtain additional evidence. This is called a remand. The ALJ will make another decision which again may be reviewed by the Appeals Council.

§ 1307 - Court Review

The Social Security Act provides that a federal district court has the authority to review any final decision of the Social Security Administration if it was rendered after a hearing. This means you must go through the administrative appeals process before going to court.

After the district court reviews your case, it can affirm, reverse or send it back to Social Security for further proceedings (remand).

The court's review is limited to determining if the decision is supported by substantial evidence or contains an error of law. If there is *any* evidence to support the decision, you will lose, unless there is a legal error. For example, if the administrative law judge chose to give more weight to one doctor's report (saying you *are not* disabled) than to another doctor's report (saying you *are* disabled), the court will uphold him. He is considered the "fact-finder," and his conclusions will not be disturbed if supported by more than a "scintilla of evidence;" i.e., such evidence as a reasonable mind might accept as adequate to support a conclusion.

If there is error in his application of the law to the facts of your case, the court may overturn his decision. Such cases may result in a remand to the administrative law judge to determine additional facts in light of the correct rule of law.

A legal action seeking review of a final decision must be filed in federal district court within 60 days. The court's filing fee is currently $60. Any legal fees must be approved by the court.

§ 1308 - Time Limits

A request for a reconsideration, hearing or Appeals Council review must be filed within 60 days of the prior decision. The time limit for filing a civil action in federal court is the same.

The time starts running from the date you receive the notice of the decision. This is presumed to be five days after the notice was mailed.

A protective filing statement (§402) will stop the running of the time limit for administrative appeals, but not for the civil action. It must indicate clearly an intent to appeal. No formal words are required, simply "I wish to appeal the decision in my case."

The time limit for requesting an administrative review may be extended if you had "good cause" for late filing, for example, if you were hospitalized or if you never received the notice of the decision.

The time limit for filing a civil action may be extended by the Appeals Council. A request for extension should be filed before the time limit expires. If not, the request may be granted if you had good cause for being late.

If a time limit expires on a Saturday, Sunday, legal holiday or a Federal nonwork day, the time limit is extended to the next following work day.

§ 1309 - Reopening Closed Cases

A decision which has become final may be reopened and revised for any reason *within 12 months* of the notice of the initial determination.

A decision may be reopened *within four years*: if new evidence is found after the initial determination; if a clerical error was made in figuring a benefit amount; if the initial determination was clearly wrong based on the evidence in file; if there is good cause.

Good cause does not exist where the only basis for reopening is a change of legal interpretation.

A determination may be reopened *at any time*: if fraud or similar fault was involved; if someone else makes a conflicting claim on the same earnings record; for survivor benefits if the worker was presumed dead and is found alive, or is now presumed dead because of unexplained absence for 7 years; if a worker's earnings record now shows that a previous denial for insufficient earnings was wrong; if an unfavorable decision was based on a clerical error apparent on the face of the evidence in file; if errors were made involving railroad employment or military wage credits causing duplicate payments or the failure to give proper credit.

§ 1310 - Attorneys

Usually you do not require an attorney to handle your Social Security affairs, although you have the right to be represented at any time. You may require an attorney if your claim has been denied or you have incurred a substantial overpayment.

Business owners who plan to claim retirement benefits should consult an attorney *before* they give any statements to Social Security (§811).

If you wish to consult or retain a lawyer, it is important to find one well versed in the area of Social Security. Few lawyers practice in this field, although the number is growing. The Bar Association in your county may be able to refer you to a suitable lawyer. Many lawyers who practice Worker's Compensation law also handle Social Security, especially disability cases.

You are responsible for the payment of your attorney's fee. Any fee for services rendered representing you must be approved by the Social Security Administration.

If you win your case, SSA will withhold 25% of any past due benefits until an approved fee has been established. Most lawyers will accept a disability case on a contingent basis. This means that no fee will be charged if the case is unsuccessful.

When a fee has been approved, SSA will pay the attorney directly out of the withheld benefits. If there is any unused balance, it will be sent to you. If the approved fee is greater than the amount withheld, the lawyer will bill you.

Sometimes an attorney may require you to pay him a retainer in advance. If so, he must hold this in escrow (set apart from his own funds) until a fee has been approved. If the approved fee is less, he must return the difference to you.

Chapter 14
Miscellaneous Provisions

§ 1401 - Supplemental Security Income (SSI)

The SSI program was established in 1974. SSI benefits are payable to the aged (65 and over), blind, and disabled who are also in need. Social Security is an insurance program. SSI is a welfare program.

Entitlement to SSI is contingent upon the amount and types of income and resources you have available to you. The income and resources of those relatives legally responsible for your support (parents of minor children, spouses) will also affect your entitlement to SSI.

The amount of SSI payments is fixed for all recipients (although many states make supplemental payments included in the SSI check) but is affected by various factors such as types and amounts of other income you receive, the value of your resources, and whether you live alone, with others, or in a nursing home or group home.

The SSI check is gold colored and is delivered on the first day of the month. Although the SSI program is administered by the Social Security Administration, the SSI payments do not come from the Social Security trust fund. The payments are made from the general revenues of the Federal Government derived from various tax payments. If you think you are eligible for SSI or require more information you should contact your local Social Security office.

§ 1402 - Black Lung Benefits

The Federal Coal Mine Health and Safety Act of 1969 established payments to coal miners who suffer from pneumoconiosis, commonly referred to as "Black Lung." Only Black Lung claims filed before July 1, 1973, are under the jurisdiction of Social Security.

All applicants filed after that date are under the jurisdiction of the Department of Labor. Social Security does maintain jurisdiction of claims filed by the *survivors* of miners who were afflicted with Black Lung.

Black Lung payments are made to coal miners who are totally disabled due to pneumoconiosis. Additional payments may be made to these miners to provide for a dependent wife, divorced wife, or children. Survivor benefits may be paid to widows, children, a surviving divorced wife, parent, brother or sister of a miner who was entitled to Black Lung benefits at the time of his death, or who was totally disabled by pneumoconiosis at the time of death, or who died from pneumoconiosis. For further information contact Social Security or the Department of Labor.

§ 1403 - Benefit Estimates

The Social Security Administration will provide an estimate of the amount of benefits payable to anyone who requests it. All benefit estimates given by Social Security will be based on the amount of earnings actually shown on the record of earnings and will not be based on any proposed future earnings. Although Social Security will provide estimates for people of any age, those estimates for workers who are under age 60 cannot be completely accurate. Estimates for people of any age can only be based on the information currently available to Social Security. Estimates of benefits far into the future have been shown to be inaccurate because of changes in the Social Security Act and wide swings in inflation.

If you are nearing retirement age and would like an estimate, you may contact your Social Security office.

§ 1404 - Obtaining Your Earnings Record

Social Security will provide, free of charge, a "Statement of Earnings." This statement shows the annual earnings credited to your record. Because of the amount of time it takes to process reports of earnings, the first and second year preceding the request may not be available. It is a good idea to check your Social Security records every three years.

§ 1405 - Correcting Your Earnings Record

Usually, the earnings record can only be corrected up to three years, three months and 15 days after the year the wages were paid or self-employment income was earned. If you have a disagreement with your employer about how much you were paid, when you were paid, or whether the work was covered under Social Security, you must act within the three years, three months and 15 day time limit. If a disagreement exists Social Security will help you obtain the necessary information to settle the dispute. Based on all evidence received, Social Security will decide whether earnings can be credited, how much earnings should be credited, and for what period. Social Security will notify you of the decision they have reached and what corrective action, if any, they are taking.

Once the three year, three month, 15 day time limit has expired, the earnings record cannot be revised unless one of the following conditions is met:

1. An entry was established through fraud;

2. A mechanical, clerical, or other obvious error is detected (such as earnings mistakenly reported under a wrong Social Security number or mistakenly unreported);

3. Earnings were credited to the wrong person or to the wrong period;

4. To transfer earnings to or from the Railroad Retirement Board if reported to the wrong agency;

5. To add wages paid by an employer who made no report of any wages paid to an employee;

6. To add or remove wages in accordance with a wage report filed by an employer;

7. To add self-employment income if the tax return was filed within the legal time limit;

8. To add self-employment income up to the amount of employee wages deleted as being erroneously reported if a self-employment tax return is filed within three years, three months and 15 days of the year the earnings were deleted. (This may occur where "employment" later is determined to be "self-employment.")

Social Security does its best to ensure that wages are properly reported. Although corrections legally can be made at a later time, the longer you wait to correct a problem, the harder it will be, due to destruction and loss of records. You should take action to correct your Social Security record as soon as a problem is identified.

§ 1406 - Reporting Change of Address

A change of address can be reported to Social Security using three methods - with a telephone call, visiting the office, or by letter.

The Department of the Treasury prepares and mails all Government checks. Social Security must notify the Treasury Department of all address changes. Social Security checks are delivered to the local post offices well in advance of the due date to ensure their timely delivery. All of these factors take time. It can require as much as 40 to 45 days for a change of address to take effect. It is important to notify Social Security as soon as you know your new address. It is also important to file a change of address form with the Post Office so that even if the change of address does not register, the Post Office will forward your check.

§ 1407 - Claim Numbers and Beneficiary Identification Codes

Every person who applies for Social Security benefits is assigned a claim number and all records are maintained by that number. The claim number consists of the Social Security number of the worker on whose account the benefits are based with a letter (or letter *and* number) following it. It is used on all correspondence from Social Security.

The retirement beneficiary's claim number is his Social Security number followed by the letter A. His wife on his account is assigned his number followed by the letter B (if she is 62 or over) or B2 (if she receives because she has a child in her care). Children are identified by the letter C and a number (usually 1 for the youngest, 2 for the next youngest, etc.). Widows receiving on account of age are identified by the letter D.

If a person is entitled on more than one account, the records are maintained under both accounts, but one account takes precedence. If a woman receives both as a retired wage earner and as a widow, all correspondence and checks will be sent to her in her own number followed by the letter A. Other than the initial award letter, the secondary account number will not be mentioned. Beneficiary identification code letters are listed at Appendix 7.

§ 1408 - Who is Entitled to Benefits Due a Deceased Beneficiary

An underpayment exists when benefits are due a person which have not been paid. Usually underpayments are due because of returned checks or increases in benefit amounts for various reasons. If the underpaid person is alive the payment is made to him (or his representative).

A deceased person can also be due an underpayment. When this occurs the underpayment is paid to whichever person is highest in priority in the following list:

1. To the widow or widower if either were living in the same household at the time of death, or entitled to monthly benefits on the same earnings record (receiving spouse's benefits).

2. To the child(ren) of the underpaid person who was entitled to monthly benefits on the same earnings record as the deceased for the month of death. The underpayment is divided equally among all such children.

3. To the parent(s) of the underpaid person entitled to monthly benefits on the same earnings record for the month of death.

4. To the widow who was neither living with the underpaid person nor entitled to monthly benefits on the same earnings record.

5. To the child(ren) who were not entitled to monthly benefits on the same earnings record as the deceased for the month of death.

6. To the parent(s) who were not entitled to monthly benefits on the same account as the deceased.

7. To the legal representative of the estate.

For example, if the deceased was survived by his wife who was living with him but not entitled to monthly Social Security benefits and an 18 year old daughter who was receiving monthly Social Security benefits on his account, the underpayment would be paid to his widow. If the deceased and his wife were separated, the underpayment would be paid to his daughter. If the daughter was not entitled to monthly benefits and no one else was, the underpayment would be payable to the widow. The underpayment is not paid to all persons on the list of priority. It is paid only to the highest person on the list. Two or more people with the same priority (e.g., two surviving children) split the underpayment equally.

If Social Security can determine who is entitled to the underpayment, they will pay it automatically without a specific request. If the Social Security records are insufficient to determine all persons who may be entitled (surviving wife or children not entitled to monthly benefits) a request is required from one person who is entitled to share in the underpayment. If the underpayment is over $400, proof of relationship may be required.

§ 1409 - Taxation of Social Security Benefits

Social Security benefits are subject to income tax if you have income which exceeds the following amounts: $25,000, if you file as a single taxpayer; $32,000, if you are married and file a joint return; but $0, if you are married and you live with your spouse at any time during the year and file separate returns.

When you figure your total Social Security benefits received, you have to include gross benefits *before* deductions for such items as the Medicare premium, a lawyer's fee, or Worker's Compensation offsets.

In figuring your total income, you must also include "non-taxable" earnings such as interest from municipal bonds. The first month's benefit subject to the tax is that for the month of December, 1983 (paid January 3, 1984). Any payments received attributable to a period before December, 1983, no matter when you receive them, are not subject to tax. The Social Security benefits are taxable only to the extent they exceed the above limits but for an individual only 50% of the excess is taxable up to $34,000, 85% of the excess over $34,000; for a couple, 50% of the excess over $32,000 up to $44,000, then 85% of the excess over $44,000.

§ 1410 - Immunity of Benefits from Creditors

No creditor has the right to attach a Social Security benefit. The Social Security benefit can only be attached by the IRS for the payment of back taxes or for child support payments. Once the benefit has been received and put into an account such as a savings account or a checking account, it can be attached unless it is a separate account clearly marked "Social Security Benefits." It is very important if you are receiving benefits on behalf of a child and placing them in a savings account that the account clearly specifies that the funds are Social Security funds, so that your creditors cannot attach the child's money.

§ 1411 - Criminal Penalties for Fraud

Under the Social Security program, fraud can be found to exist if a person furnishes false information as to identity to get a Social Security number, or a false statement in connection with a claim for Social Security benefits, or if a person uses a Social Security number obtained by fraud.

Fraud can also be found if a person conceals or fails to report any event affecting the right of a person to receive a Social Security check, or uses Social Security benefits received on behalf of one person for the use of somebody other than that person. Social Security may prosecute fraud even if no benefits were ever paid by the government on the basis of the statement.

The penalty for fraud ranges from a minimum of not more than a $500 fine or imprisonment of one year or both, to a fine of not more than $10,000 or imprisonment for up to 15 years or both. Acts such as alleging you retired when you actually have not or alleging that you transferred a business to your spouse when you did not are a few examples of cases Social Security may prosecute.

§ 1412 - Foreign Social Security Credit

Social Security has entered into agreement with 17 foreign countries: Austria, Belgium, Canada, Finland, France, Germany, Greece, Ireland, Italy, Luxembourg, Netherlands, Norway, Portugal, Spain, Sweden, Switzerland and United Kingdom. The agreements allow people who have work credit in those countries to file an application with Social Security in the United States for potential Social Security benefits from the other country. This provision allows some people who don't have enough work under either Social Security system to be able to collect one Social Security benefit. It also allows people who are entitled to benefits from both systems to file for them and collect them conveniently.

At the time you file for Social Security benefits in the U.S., the interviewer will ask if you ever worked in a foreign country covered by the agreement. Social Security will complete a second application for potential benefits from that other country for you.

§ 1413 - Railroad Employment

People who work for the railroads are not covered under Social Security, they are covered by the Railroad Retirement Board (RRB). If you are entitled to benefits from both Social Security and from the RRB, they are made in one combined payment. SSA will compute your Social Security benefit and send the information to the RRB who will figure your annuity and adjust it for the amount of Social Security you receive. To be entitled to railroad retirement benefits, an employee must have ten years of railroad service. If he has less, his railroad employment will be credited to his Social Security account. If an employee does not have enough work to collect a Social Security payment, his earnings under Social Security will be credited to his railroad retirement account. Survivor benefits may be paid by either agency.

More information on railroad retirement benefits can be obtained by writing to Information Service, U.S. Railroad Retirement Board, 844 Rush Street, Chicago, Illinois 60611, or by contacting Railroad Retirement Board officials in major cities throughout the country.

§ 1414 - Receiving Benefits for Someone Else

Social Security benefits will be paid to an adult in his own name unless he has been shown to be incompetent or incapable of managing his own funds. A mentally ill person may still be able to manage benefits in his own interest; if so the payment will be made directly to him. A physically disabled person will have payments made to a representative payee only if he is so disabled as to be unable to manage benefit payments even with the help of someone else. Benefits to children under the age of 18 normally are made to a representative payee. The payment may be made directly to a child under the age of 18 if the child is entirely self-supporting and living away from home, or in other limited circumstances. It is unusual for a child under the age of 18 to collect payments on his own behalf. Once a child turns 18, payments are made directly to him, unless there is a need for a representative payee.

The order of preference in appointing a representative payee for a child is: (1) the natural or adoptive parent with custody or a court appointed guardian; (2) the natural or adoptive parent who does not have custody of the child but who contributes to the child's support and demonstrates strong concern for the child's wellbeing; (3) a natural or adoptive parent who demonstrates a strong concern for the child's wellbeing; (4) a relative, including a stepparent, having custody of the child; (5) a relative who does not have custody of the child but who contributes to the child's support and demonstrates a strong concern for the child's wellbeing; (6) an authorized social agency; and (7) a relative or close friend who demonstrates strong concern for the child's wellbeing.

The order of preference for an adult is (1) the legal guardian, spouse or other relative who has actual custody of the beneficiary or who demonstrates a strong concern for his welfare; (2) a friend who has custody, who demonstrates a strong concern for his welfare; (3) a public or non-profit agency or institution having custody of the beneficiary; and (4) a private institution operating for profit licensed under applicable state law having custody of the beneficiary such as a nursing home.

The responsibilities of a representative payee are: to apply benefit payments for the beneficiary's use; to maintain a concern for the personal welfare of the beneficiary; to notify Social Security when the responsibility for the welfare and care of any person entitled to Social Security ends; to report to Social Security any changes that may affect the beneficiary's right to receive Social Security; and to give Social Security periodic written reports accounting for the use of benefits, if requested to do so. Benefits paid to a representative payee must be spent for the beneficiary's current needs or saved for the beneficiary if all current needs are being met.

If you receive Social Security benefits on behalf of another and find that you are able to save some to establish a bank account for the person, the bank account must clearly indicate that the funds in that account are Social Security benefits. The preferred format for the title of the account is: "Name of Beneficiary, By Name of Representative Payee," or "Name of Beneficiary, By Name of Representative Payee, Trustee." A bank account title such as "Name of Payee in Trust for Beneficiary" should not be used because some states treat the funds in such an account as belonging to the Representative Payee. Whatever the title of the account is, it must clearly indicate that the money in the account is the property of the beneficiary, and no one else, and that it is Social Security benefits.

Social Security requires a written account from representative payees on a periodic basis. If you are acting as a representative payee, you should keep records showing how the Social Security money was spent. The reporting they will ask you for may include the amount of benefits you had at the beginning of the period, where the beneficiary lived during the period, the amount of income from other sources during the year, how the benefits were spent, how much of the Social Security benefits were saved and how they were invested.

Appendices

Appendix 1
List of Secondary Proof of Age
(see §410)

If *no* birth certificate or baptismal certificate recorded before age 5 is available, Social Security requires you to submit other documents to prove your age. This appendix is divided into 2 sections - First Priority Convincing Records and Second Priority Convincing Records.

I - First Priority Convincing Records

If you submit *one* document from the list and the date of birth on that document agrees with the date of birth you gave Social Security when you applied for your Social Security Number, no other proof of age is necessary.

I-1. Family Bible or other family record recorded before age 36.

I-2. School or School Census records recorded before age 21.

I-3. 1910, 1920, or 1930 Federal Census record.

I-4. Domestic or Canadian delayed birth record established before age 55.

I-5. State census records for 1905 or 1915.

I-6. Insurance Policies taken out before age 21.

I-7. Immigration and Naturalization Service (INS) arrival records recorded before age 31.

I-8. Religious records recorded before age 18.

I-9. Newspaper birth announcements.

II - Second Priority Convincing Records

If no First Priority Convincing Record (above) is available (as well as no birth or baptismal record recorded before age 5) and you submit *one* document from this list, if the date of birth on that document agrees with the date of birth you gave Social Security when you applied for your Social Security Number, no other proof of age is necessary.

II-1.   School records recorded after age 20 and before age 55.

II-2.   Baptismal record recorded after age 17 and before age 55.

II-3.   1925 State census records.

II-4.   Domestic or Canadian delayed birth record established after age 54 - if the delayed birth record shows the basis for the date of birth.

II-5.   Birth records for your children recorded before you were age 31.

II-6.   Marriage records recorded before age 36.

II-7.   Citizenship data recorded before age 26.

II-8.   World War II draft and discharge records recorded before age 31.

II-9.   Employment records established before age 21.

II-10. Voting records established before age 56.

II-11. Other records recorded before age 21.

Appendix 2
Quarters of Coverage Required for Insured Status

Following is a chart showing the earnings required for a Quarter of Coverage and 4 charts which show the minimum number of Quarters of Coverage needed for Insured Status, according to the type of benefit.

Chart 1: Earnings Required for a Quarter of Coverage

Year	Amount
Pre-1978	$ 50
1978	250
1979	260
1980	290
1981	310
1982	340
1983	370
1984	390
1985	410
1986	440
1987	460
1988	470
1989	500
1990	520
1991	540
1992	570
1993	590
1994	620
1995	630
1996	640

Chart 2: Retirement Benefits

Year of Birth	Minimum Number of Quarters
1915	26
1916	27
1917	28
1918	29
1919	30
1920	31
1921	32

Year of Birth	Minimum Number of Quarters
1922	33
1923	34
1924	35
1925	36
1926	37
1927	38
1928	39
1929 and later	40

Chart 3: Disability or Survivor Benefits for People Born Before 1930

Year of Onset of Disability or Death	Minimum Number of Quarters of Coverage Required
1970	19
1971	20
1972	21
1973	22
1974	23
1975	24
1976	25
1977	26
1978	27
1979	28
1980	29
1981	30
1982	31
1983	32
1984	33
1985	34
1986	35
1987	36
1988	37
1989	38
1990	39
1991 and later	40

Chart 4: Disability or Survivor Benefits
for People Born in 1930 or Later

Age of Onset of Disability or Death	Minimum Number of Quarters of Coverage Required
28 and younger	6
29	7
30	8
31	9
32	10
33	11
34	12
35	13
36	14
37	15
38	16
39	17
40	18
41	19
42	20
43	21
44	22
45	23
46	24
47	25
48	26
49	27
50	28
51	29
52	30
53	31
54	32
55	33
56	34
57	35
58	36
59	37
60	38
61	39
62 and older	40

Chart 5: Disability Insured Status
(see §604)

Note: This chart shows the minimum number of quarters of coverage required in the calendar quarters immediately preceding onset of disability. For example, 15/30 means that 15 quarters of coverage are needed in the 30 calendar quarters (7-1/2 years) before onset of disability. 20/40 means that 20 quarters of coverage are needed in the 40 calendar quarters (10 years before onset of disability).

Age at Onset of Disability	Minimum Number of Quarters of Coverage Required/Calendar Quarters Before Disability
24 and younger	6/12
24-1/2	7/14
25	8/16
25-1/2	9/18
26	10/20
26-1/2	11/22
27	12/24
27-1/2	13/26
28	14/28
28-1/2	15/30
29	16/32
29-1/2	17/34
30	18/36
30-1/2	19/38
31	20/40

Appendix 3
FICA Yearly Maximums
(Maximum Earnings Subject to Social Security Tax)

Year	Earnings
1937 through 1950	$ 3,000
1951 through 1954	3,600
1955 through 1958	4,200
1959 through 1965	4,800
1966 through 1967	6,600
1968 through 1971	7,800
1972	9,000
1973	10,800
1974	13,200
1975	14,100
1976	15,300
1977	16,500
1978	17,700
1979	22,900
1980	25,900
1981	29,700
1982	32,400
1983	35,700
1984	37,800
1985	39,600
1986	42,000
1987	43,800
1988	45,000
1989	48,000
1990	51,300
1991	53,400
1992	55,500
1993	57,600
1994	60,600
1995	61,200
1996	62,700

Future maximums will be increased based on the rate of inflation and announced by the Social Security Administration in the fall of the preceding year.

Appendix 4
Reduction Factors (§§707 - 710)

Chart 1: Retirement Benefits

Reduction Months	Reduction Factor	Reduction Months	Reduction Factor
1	.994	19	.894
2	.988	20	.888
3	.983	21	.883
4	.977	22	.877
5	.972	23	.872
6	.966	24	.866
7	.961	25	.861
8	.955	26	.855
9	.950	27	.850
10	.944	28	.844
11	.938	29	.838
12	.933	30	.833
13	.927	31	.827
14	.922	32	.822
15	.916	33	.816
16	.911	34	.811
17	.905	35	.805
18	.900	36	.800

Chart 2: Wife's Benefits

Reduction Months	Reduction Factor	Reduction Months	Reduction Factor
1	.993	19	.868
2	.986	20	.861
3	.979	21	.854
4	.972	22	.847
5	.965	23	.840
6	.958	24	.833
7	.951	25	.826
8	.944	26	.819
9	.937	27	.812
10	.930	28	.805
11	.923	29	.798
12	.916	30	.791
13	.909	31	.784

Reduction Months	Reduction Factor	Reduction Months	Reduction Factor
14	.902	32	.777
15	.895	33	.770
16	.888	34	.763
17	.881	35	.756
18	.875	36	.750

Chart 3: Widow's Benefits

Reduction Months	Reduction Factor	Reduction Months	Reduction Factor
1	.995	31	.853
2	.991	32	.848
3	.986	33	.843
4	.981	34	.839
5	.976	35	.834
6	.972	36	.829
7	.967	37	.824
8	.962	38	.820
9	.957	39	.815
10	.953	40	.810
11	.948	41	.805
12	.943	42	.801
13	.938	43	.796
14	.934	44	.791
15	.929	45	.786
16	.924	46	.782
17	.919	47	.777
18	.915	48	.772
19	.910	49	.767
20	.905	50	.763
21	.900	51	.758
22	.896	52	.753
23	.891	53	.748
24	.886	54	.744
25	.881	55	.739
26	.877	56	.734
27	.872	57	.729
28	.867	58	.725
29	.862	59	.720
30	.858	60	.715

Appendix 5: Cost of Living Increases

Year	Percentage	Year	Percentage
1992	3.7%	1995	2.8%
1993	3.0%	1996	2.6%
1994	2.6%		

Appendix 6: Earnings Limits by Year

Year	Age	Monthly	Yearly
1992	Under 65	$620	$ 7,440
	65 and Older	850	10,200
1993	Under 65	640	7,680
	65 and Older	880	10,560
1994	Under 65	670	8,040
	65 and Older	930	11,160
1995	Under 65	680	8,160
	65 and Older	940	11,280
1996	Under 65	690	8,280
	65 and Older	960	11,520

Appendix 7:
List of Most Common Beneficiary Identification Codes

A - Retirement on own work record

B - Aged Wife

B1 - Aged Husband

B2 - Young Wife (with child in care)

B6 - Divorced Wife

C - Child

D - Aged Widow

D1 - Aged Widower

D6 - Surviving Divorced Wife

E - Young Widow (mother)

E1 - Surviving Divorced Mother

E4 - Young Widower (father)

F - Parent

G - Lump Sum Claimant

HA - Disabled Worker

HB - Aged Wife of Disabled Worker

HB2 - Young Wife of Disabled Worker

HC - Child of Disabled Worker

J - Prouty (special age 72 benefits)

K - Prouty (wife)

M - Medicare-Medical Insurance Only

T - Medicare Only - Both Parts

W - Disabled Widow

W1 - Disabled Widower

W6 - Surviving Disabled Divorced Wife

Appendix 8
Program Service Centers

These centers store folders and work on certain cases after they have been processed by a District Office. See discussion in §102. Cases are assigned based on the first three digits of the social security claim number. Disability cases where the worker is under 59-1/2 go to the Office of Disability Operations (PSC-7). Cases where the claimant lives abroad are handled by the Division of International Operations (PSC-8).

Program Service Center No. & Initials	Social Security Account Number Breakdown (1st 3 digits)	Mailing Address
PSC-1 (NEPSC)	001-134	DHHS Social Security Administration Northeastern Program Service Center 96-05 Horace Harding Expressway Flushing, NY 11368
PSC-2 (MATPSC)	135-222 232-236 577-584	DHHS Social Security Administration Mid-Atlantic Program Service Center 300 Spring Garden St. Philadelphia, PA 19123
PSC-3 (SEPC)	223-231 237-267 400-428 587	DHHS Social Security Administration Southeastern Program Service Center 2001 12th Ave. N. Birmingham, AL 35285
PSC-4 (GLPSC)	268-302 316-399 700 series	DHHS Social Security Administration Great Lakes Program Service Center 600 W. Madison St. Chicago, IL 60606

Program Service Center No. & Initials	Social Security Account Number Breakdown (1st 3 digits)	Mailing Address

PSC-5 (WNPSC)	501-504
	516-524
	526-576
	586
		DHHS
		Social Security
		  Administration
		Western Program
		  Service Center
		BX 2000
		Richmond, CA 94802

PSC-6 (MAMPSC)	303-315
	429-500
	505-515
	525
	585
		DHHS
		Social Security
		  Administration
		Mid-America Program
		  Service Center
		601 E. 12th Street
		Kansas City, MO 64106

PSC-7 (ODO)	All disability and end stage renal disease cases (under age 59-1/2)	DHHS
		Social Security
		  Administration
		Office of Disability
		  Operations
		Baltimore, MD 21241

PSC-8 (DIO)	Foreign Claims	Social Security
		  Administration
		Division of
		  International
		  Operations
		BX 1756
		Baltimore, MD 21203

Appendix 9: Form SSA-735

DEPARTMENT OF HEALTH AND HUMAN SERVICES
SOCIAL SECURITY ADMINISTRATION

TOE 540

NOTICE OF MISSING SOCIAL SECURITY PAYMENT

This refers to your inquiry about a missing payment. If the payment is still missing, please complete the other side of this card and return it in the preaddressed envelope. No postage is needed.
NO FURTHER ACTION WILL BE TAKEN ON THE PAYMENT UNLESS THIS CARD IS COMPLETED, SIGNED, AND RETURNED.
If you receive the payment before you hear from the Treasury Department, please notify the Social Security Office.

Social Security Office

FINANCIAL ORGANIZATION

Name

Address

Zip Code

Routing and Transit Number

"C" if checking, or "S" if savings | Depositor's Account Number

Form SSA-735 (3-84)

GPO : 1988 O - 214-194

Name of Payee to whom missing payment is due (*Please Print*)	Social Security Claim Number

DATE OF PAYMENT

Payment for: ☐ Social Security ☐ Supplemental Security Income ☐ Black Lung

The above described payment was → *(check applicable box)*

☐ Not Received   (a) Received, but ☐ Destroyed ☐ Lost ☐ Stolen   (b) *Was it endorsed?* ☐ Yes ☐ No

ANYONE WHO MAKES A FALSE CLAIM COMMITS A CRIME PUNISHABLE UNDER FEDERAL LAW and can be FINED not more than $10,000 OR IMPRISONED not more than five years, OR BOTH. (Title 18 USCS, Sec. 287, U.S. Code)

Have you changed your mailing address ☐ YES ☐ NO

Current Mailing Address (*Include Zip Code*)

I/we wish to make formal claim to the Treasury Department for stoppage of payment and the issuance of a substitute payment. *(Both husband and wife must sign if co-payees of a combined payment.) (Please note information on reverse side.)*

SIGNATURE OF PAYEE

Date   Payee's telephone number (*area code*)

SIGNATURE OF CO-PAYEE OR FINANCIAL ORGANIZATION REPRESENTATIVE

Form SSA-735 (3-84)

Appendix 10
Effect of Marriage of One
Beneficiary to Another (see §904)

Type of Beneficiary	Effect of Marriage to Another Beneficiary
I. Retired Worker (§202) Disabled Worker (§203) Widow(er) (§207) Disabled Widow(er) (§209) Surviving Divorced Spouse (divorced widow(er)) (§210) Disabled Surviving Divorced Spouse (divorced widow(er) (§210)	No effect, benefits continue
II. Divorced Spouse (§206) Parent (§215)	Benefits terminate if marriage is to a Retired or Disabled Worker, or a Child under 18 or in school; if marriage is to any other beneficiary, benefits continue.
III. Mother/Father (young widow(er)) (§208) Divorced Mother/Father (§210) Disabled Adult Child (§213)	Benefits terminate if marriage to a Child under 18 or in school (Child's benefits also terminate); if marriage is to any other beneficiary, benefits continue.
IV. Child under 18 or in School (§§211-212)	Benefits terminate upon remarriage to anyone.

Appendix 11
Delayed Retirement Credits

The amount of a Delayed Retirement Credit is calculated as a percentage of the Primary Insurance Amount, based on the number of months no benefit is received after age 65 due to excess earnings. The percentages listed are annual. The credit for each month is 1/12 of the annual figure. The amount of the credit is based on year of birth.

Year of Birth	Annual Credit
1917-24	3%
1925-26	3.5%
1927-28	4.0%
1929-30	4.5%
1931-32	5%
1933-34	5.5%
1935-36	6%
1937-38	6.5%
1939-40	7.0%
1941-42	7.5%
1943 and later	8.0%

Appendix 12
Medicare Premiums and Deductibles

	1995	1996
Hospital Insurance		
Premium - Part A		$261
$289		
Medical Insurance		
Premium - Part B	$46.10	$42.50 *
* legislation proposed to amend this amount		
Hospital Insurance - Part A		
Co-Payments		
First 60 Days (Total)	$716	$736
61st-90th Day (per day)	$179	$184
Lifetime Reserve (per day)	$358	$368
Skilled Nursing Care		
20-100th day (per day)	$89.50	$92
Medical Insurance - Part B		
Yearly Deductible	$100	$100

Index

National titles valid in all 50 States

Social Security Benefits Handbook 14.95
Jurors' Rights 9.95
Legal Malpractice and Other Claims Against Your Lawyer . 18.95
Living Trusts & Simple Ways to Avoid Probate 19.95
Simple Ways to Protect Yourself From Lawsuits .. 24.95
Help Your Lawyer Win Your Case 12.95
The Most Valuable Business Forms You'll Ever Need 19.95
Debtors' Rights, A Legal Self-Help Guide, 2nd Ed. ... 12.95
Grandparents' Rights 19.95
Divorces From Hell 10.95
Legal Research Made Easy 14.95
The Most Valuable Corporate Forms You'll Ever Need 24.95
How to Register Your Own Copyright 19.95
How to Register Your Own Trademark 19.95

Lawsuits of the Rich & Famous 10.95
How to File Your Own Bankruptcy, 3rd Ed. 19.95
U.S.A. Immigration Guide 19.95
Guia de Inmigración a Estados Unidos 19.95
Victims' Rights 12.95
How to File Your Own Divorce 19.95
How to Write Your Own Premarital Agreement ... 19.95
How to Form Your Own Corporation 19.95
How to Negotiate Real Estate Contracts, 2nd Ed. . 14.95
How to Negotiate Real Estate Leases. 2nd Ed. 14.95
Neighbor vs. Neighbor 12.95
The Power of Attorney Handbook 19.95
Successful Real Estate Brokerage Management 19.95

Florida Legal Guides

How to File for Divorce in Florida, 4th Ed. 19.95
Landlords' Rights & Duties in Florida, 5th Ed. 19.95
How to Modify Your Florida Divorce Judgment, 2nd Ed. 19.95
How to Form a Simple Corporation in Florida, 3rd Ed. 19.95
How to Form a Nonprofit Corporation in Florida, 3rd Ed. 19.95
How to Win in Florida Small Claims Court, 5th Ed. 14.95
How to Probate an Estate in Florida, 2nd Ed. 24.95
How to Start a Business in Florida, 4th Ed. 16.95
How to File a Florida Construction Lien, 2nd Ed. 19.95
Land Trusts in Florida, 4th Ed. 24.95
How to Make a Florida Will, 3rd Ed. 9.95
How to Change Your Name in Florida, 3rd Ed. 14.95
Florida Power of Attorney Handbook 9.95
How to File for Guardianship in Florida 19.95
How to File an Adoption in Florida 19.95
Winning in Florida Traffic Court 14.95
Women's Legal Rights in Florida 19.95

Southeastern Region

•Alabama •Georgia •Mississippi •South Carolina
•Florida •Louisiana •North Carolina •Texas

How to Register Your Own Trademark (S.E. Ed.)	$21.95
How to Form Your Own Partnership (S.E. Ed.)	$19.95

Texas

How to File for Divorce in Texas	$19.95
How to Make a Texas Will	$ 9.95
How to Start a Business in Texas	$16.95
Landlords' Rights & Duties in Texas	$19.95
How to Probate an Estate in Texas	$19.95
How to Form a Simple Corporation in Texas	$19.95
How to Win in Small Claims Court in Texas	$14.95

Minnesota

How to File for Divorce in Minnesota	$19.95
How to Make a Minnesota Will	$ 9.95
How to Start a Business in Minnesota	$16.95
How to Form a Simple Corporation in Minnesota	$19,95

Michigan

How to File for Divorce in Michigan	$19.95
How to Make a Michigan Will	$ 9.95
How to Start a Business in Michigan	$16.95

North Carolina

How to File for Divorce in North Carolina	$19.95
How to Make a North Carolina Will	$ 9.95
How to Start a Business in North Carolina	$16.95

Georgia

How to File for Divorce in Georgia	$19.95
How to Make a Georgia Will	$ 9.95
How to Start and Run a Georgia Business	$ 16.95

Alabama

How to File for Divorce in Alabama	$19.95
How to Make an Alabama Will	$ 9.95
How to Start a Business in Alabama	$16.95

South Carolina

How to File for Divorce in South Carolina	$19.95
How to Make a South Carolina Will	$ 9.95
How to Start a Business in South Carolina	$16.95

Order Form

To order these publications, please send this form with check or money order to: Sourcebooks, Inc., P.O. Box 372, Naperville, IL 60566.

Prices subject to change

☐ Check Enclosed

☐ Money Order Enclosed

For **Credit Card Orders** call:

1-800-226-5291

or fax this form to 1-800-408-3291

We accept VISA, MasterCard, &American Express:

Card number: ☐☐☐☐☐☐☐☐☐☐☐☐☐☐☐☐

Expiration date: ☐☐☐☐

Ship to:

Name_____

Address_____

City_____

State_____ Zip_____

☐ American Express   ☐ Visa
☐ MasterCard

VISA   **MasterCard**   American Express

Quantity	Title	Unit Price	Total Price
	Subtotal		
	Sales Tax (CA, FL & IL residents only)		
	*Shipping		
	Total		

Signature

*Shipping: $4.00 (1 book); add $1.00 for each additional book.